HIGHER SCORES ON

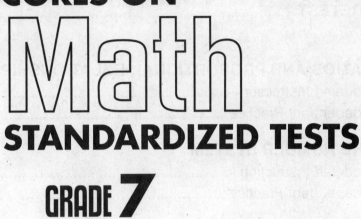

Math
STANDARDIZED TESTS
GRADE 7

Contents

Introduction

Welcome to *Higher Scores on Math Standardized Tests*, Grade 7. You have selected a book that will help your student develop the skills he or she needs to succeed on the standardized math tests. The items in this workbook have been closely aligned to the Common Core State Standards for Mathematics, which cover grade-level skills for mathematics.

Although testing can be a source of anxiety for students, this book will give your student the preparation and practice that he or she needs to feel better prepared and more confident when taking standardized math tests. Research shows that students who are acquainted with the scoring format of standardized tests score higher on those tests. Students also score higher when they practice and understand the skills and objectives covered on the tests.

This book has many features that will help you prepare your student to take standardized math tests:
- Modeled instruction about how to answer test questions and hints to guide the student toward the correct response
- Test-taking tips
- Pretest and Practice tests in a standardized test format
- A complete answer key, including references to the specific Common Core State Standards being tested
- A correlation of the Common Core State Standards to the questions

If your student expresses anxiety about taking a test or completing these lessons, help him or her understand what causes the stress. Then, talk about ways to eliminate anxiety. Above all, enjoy this time you spend with your student. He or she will feel your support, and test scores will improve as success in test taking is experienced. Help your student maintain a positive attitude about taking a standardized test. Let him or her know that each test provides an opportunity to shine.

Multiple-Choice Items

Multiple-choice items will be familiar to students from other experiences. For multiple-choice items, four answer choices are given. The item itself may be a multi-step problem.

To help students succeed with multiple-choice items:
- Have students solve the problem first.
- Have students find the answer choice that matches their solution.
- Once the correct answer has been identified, demonstrate how to mark the answer.

What if no answer matches?
- Have students consider that Not Here may be the correct answer.
- Have students restate the problem in their own words to determine the source of the error.
- Have students evaluate each answer choice to eliminate ones that do not fit the problem.
- Have volunteers demonstrate how they solved multiple-choice problems.

Common Core State Standards for Mathematics Correlation Chart

Standard	Descriptor	Pretest	Lessons	Practice Test A	Practice Test B
	Ratios and Proportional Relationships				
	Analyze proportional relationships and use them to solve real-world and mathematical problems.				
7.RP.1	Compute unit rates associated with ratios of fractions, including ratios of lengths, areas and other quantities measured in like or different units. *For example, if a person walks $\frac{1}{2}$ mile in each $\frac{1}{4}$ hour, compute the unit rate as the complex fraction $\frac{\frac{1}{2}}{\frac{1}{4}}$ miles per hour, equivalently 2 miles per hour.*	4, 11	2, 6, 13, 14, 15, 27, 31, 34, 40, 45, 46, 50, 53, 62	2, 26	22, 57
7.RP.2	Recognize and represent proportional relationships between quantities.				
7.RP.2.a	Decide whether two quantities are in a proportional relationship, e.g., by testing for equivalent ratios in a table or graphing on a coordinate plane and observing whether the graph is a straight line through the origin.	6, 7	8, 21, 22, 23, 29, 30, 43, 48, 52, 63, 64, 67	48, 58	3, 54
7.RP.2.b	Identify the constant of proportionality (unit rate) in tables, graphs, equations, diagrams, and verbal descriptions of proportional relationships.	3	3, 10, 17, 24, 37, 39, 47, 51, 58, 65, 68, 75	16, 31	5, 21
7.RP.2.c	Represent proportional relationships by equations. *For example, if total cost t is proportional to the number n of items purchased at a constant price p, the relationship between the total cost and the number of items can be expressed as t = pn.*	1, 8	5, 7, 18, 20, 36, 44, 49, 54, 55, 60, 70, 74	8, 35	6, 43
7.RP.2.d	Explain what a point (x, y) on the graph of a proportional relationship means in terms of the situation, with special attention to the points (0, 0) and (1, r) where r is the unit rate.	9, 10	1, 4, 9, 11, 26, 28, 35, 42, 57, 59, 61, 72	20, 41	34, 47
7.RP.3	Use proportional relationships to solve multistep ratio and percent problems. Examples: simple interest, tax, markups and markdowns, gratuities and commissions, fees, percent increase and decrease, percent error.	2, 5, 12	12, 16, 19, 25, 32, 33, 38, 41, 56, 66, 69, 71, 73	15, 45	31, 42

Correlation Chart
Higher Scores on Math, Grade 7

Standard	Descriptor	Pretest	Lessons	Practice Test A	Practice Test B
	The Number System				
	Apply and extend previous understandings of operations with fractions to add, subtract, multiply, and divide rational numbers.				
7.NS.1	Apply and extend previous understandings of addition and subtraction to add and subtract rational numbers; represent addition and subtraction on a horizontal or vertical number line diagram.				
7.NS.1.a	Describe situations in which opposite quantities combine to make 0. *For example, a hydrogen atom has 0 charge because its two constituents are oppositely charged.*	13	5, 10, 32, 40, 55, 62, 72	57	35
7.NS.1.b	Understand $p + q$ as the number located a distance $|q|$ from p, in the positive or negative direction depending on whether q is positive or negative. Show that a number and its opposite have a sum of 0 (are additive inverses). Interpret sums of rational numbers by describing real-world contexts.	14	4, 12, 17, 26, 36, 37, 66, 67, 73	1	48
7.NS.1.c	Understand subtraction of rational numbers as adding the additive inverse, $p - q = p + (-q)$. Show that the distance between two rational numbers on the number line is the absolute value of their difference, and apply this principle in real-world contexts.	18	16, 20, 22, 38, 49, 58, 68, 69	59	12
7.NS.1.d	Apply properties of operations as strategies to add and subtract rational numbers.	19	3, 11, 13, 34, 44, 53, 56, 60, 65	7, 51	30
7.NS.2	Apply and extend previous understandings of multiplication and division and of fractions to multiply and divide rational numbers.				
7.NS.2.a	Understand that multiplication is extended from fractions to rational numbers by requiring that operations continue to satisfy the properties of operations, particularly the distributive property, leading to products such as $(-1)(-1) = 1$ and the rules for multiplying signed numbers. Interpret products of rational numbers by describing real-world contexts.	16	6, 9, 18, 27, 42, 43, 47, 64	29	17, 59
7.NS.2.b	Understand that integers can be divided, provided that the divisor is not zero, and every quotient of integers (with non-zero divisor) is a rational number. If p and q are integers, then $-\left(\frac{p}{q}\right) = \frac{(-p)}{q} = \frac{p}{(-q)}$. Interpret quotients of rational numbers by describing real-world contexts.	21	1, 8, 14, 29, 33, 51, 54, 59	22	25, 29
7.NS.2.c	Apply properties of operations as strategies to multiply and divide rational numbers.	15, 22	7, 16, 19, 30, 50, 57, 61, 70	27	24, 49

Standard	Descriptor	Pretest	Lessons	Practice Test A	Practice Test B
7.NS.2.d	Convert a rational number to a decimal using long division; know that the decimal form of a rational number terminates in 0s or eventually repeats.	17, 20	2, 21, 24, 28, 35, 41, 48, 63, 75	10, 12	36
7.NS.3	Solve real-world and mathematical problems involving the four operations with rational numbers.	23, 24	15, 23, 25, 31, 39, 45, 52, 71, 74	25, 46	7
	Expressions and Equations				
	Use properties of operations to generate equivalent expressions.				
7.EE.1	Apply properties of operations as strategies to add, subtract, factor, and expand linear expressions with rational coefficients.	25, 30, 36	7, 10, 16, 19, 23, 29, 30, 37, 42, 44, 46, 49, 55, 57, 73	4, 54	32, 33
7.EE.2	Understand that rewriting an expression in different forms in a problem context can shed light on the problem and how the quantities in it are related. *For example, $a + 0.05a = 1.05a$ means that "increase by 5%" is the same as "multiply by 1.05."*	26, 31	3, 6, 11, 17, 20, 26, 31, 35, 53, 58, 60, 61, 62, 65, 71, 72, 75	3, 40	10, 13, 14
	Solve real-life and mathematical problems using numerical and algebraic expressions and equations.				
7.EE.3	Solve multi-step real-life and mathematical problems posed with positive and negative rational numbers in any form (whole numbers, fractions, and decimals), using tools strategically. Apply properties of operations to calculate with numbers in any form; convert between forms as appropriate; and assess the reasonableness of answers using mental computation and estimation strategies. *For example: If a woman making $25 an hour gets a 10% raise, she will make an additional $\frac{1}{10}$ of her salary an hour, or $2.50, for a new salary of $27.50. If you want to place a towel bar $9\frac{3}{4}$ inches long in the center of a door that is $27\frac{1}{2}$ inches wide, you will need to place the bar about 9 inches from each edge; this estimate can be used as a check on the exact computation.*	27, 32	1, 8, 13, 18, 21, 28, 36, 38, 41, 47, 52, 54, 59, 70, 74	17, 50	4, 23, 38
7.EE.4	Use variables to represent quantities in a real-world or mathematical problem, and construct simple equations and inequalities to solve problems by reasoning about the quantities.				

Standard	Descriptor	Pretest	Lessons	Practice Test A	Practice Test B
7.EE.4.a	Solve word problems leading to equations of the form $px + q = r$ and $p(x + q) = r$, where p, q, and r are specific rational numbers. Solve equations of these forms fluently. Compare an algebraic solution to an arithmetic solution, identifying the sequence of the operations used in each approach. *For example, the perimeter of a rectangle is 54 cm. Its length is 6 cm. What is its width?*	28, 33	4, 5, 12, 14, 22, 27, 32, 34, 35, 40, 43, 56, 63, 66, 67, 68	9, 13, 18	26, 53
7.EE.4.b	Solve word problems leading to inequalities of the form $px + q > r$ or $px + q < r$, where p, q, and r are specific rational numbers. Graph the solution set of the inequality and interpret it in the context of the problem. *For example: As a salesperson, you are paid $50 per week plus $3 per sale. This week you want your pay to be at least $100. Write an inequality for the number of sales you need to make, and describe the solutions.*	29, 34	2, 9, 15, 24, 25, 33, 39, 45, 48, 50, 51, 64, 69	32, 38, 60	20, 44
	Geometry				
	Draw, construct, and describe geometrical figures and describe the relationships between them.				
7.G.1	Solve problems involving scale drawings of geometric figures, including computing actual lengths and areas from a scale drawing and reproducing a scale drawing at a different scale.	37, 43	6, 11, 13, 20, 30, 41, 45, 51, 54, 58, 63, 65	34, 37	1, 19
7.G.2	Draw (freehand, with ruler and protractor, and with technology) geometric shapes with given conditions. Focus on constructing triangles from three measures of angles or sides, noticing when the conditions determine a unique triangle, more than one triangle, or no triangle.	38, 44	14, 22, 25, 26, 28, 32, 47, 53, 62, 75	5, 43	50, 55
7.G.3	Describe the two-dimensional figures that result from slicing three-dimensional figures, as in plane sections of right rectangular prisms and right rectangular pyramids.	39, 45	5, 12, 16, 21, 29, 38, 39, 40, 43, 56	36, 47	8, 27
	Solve real-life and mathematical problems involving angle measure, area, surface area, and volume.				
7.G.4	Know the formulas for the area and circumference of a circle and use them to solve problems; give an informal derivation of the relationship between the circumference and area of a circle.	40, 46	2, 10, 17, 18, 31, 36, 42, 48, 49, 52, 57, 71, 73	44, 49	37, 39
7.G.5	Use facts about supplementary, complementary, vertical, and adjacent angles in a multi-step problem to write and solve simple equations for an unknown angle in a figure.	41, 47	3, 8, 19, 23, 24, 34, 37, 44, 55, 60, 64, 66, 69, 70	21, 33	46, 60

Standard	Descriptor	Pretest	Lessons	Practice Test A	Practice Test B
7.G.6	Solve real-world and mathematical problems involving area, volume, and surface area of two- and three-dimensional objects composed of triangles, quadrilaterals, polygons, cubes, and right prisms.	42, 48	1, 4, 7, 9, 15, 27, 33, 35, 46, 50, 59, 61, 67, 68, 72, 74	11, 19	40, 58
	Statistics and Probability				
	Use random sampling to draw inferences about a population.				
7.SP.1	Understand that statistics can be used to gain information about a population by examining a sample of the population; generalizations about a population from a sample are valid only if the sample is representative of that population. Understand that random sampling tends to produce representative samples and support valid inferences.	49	1, 14, 22, 28, 48, 50, 59, 63	14	45
7.SP.2	Use data from a random sample to draw inferences about a population with an unknown characteristic of interest. Generate multiple samples (or simulated samples) of the same size to gauge the variation in estimates or predictions. *For example, estimate the mean word length in a book by randomly sampling words from the book; predict the winner of a school election based on randomly sampled survey data. Gauge how far off the estimate or prediction might be.*	50	8, 10, 24, 42, 44, 57, 68, 75	53	11
	Draw informal comparative inferences about two populations.				
7.SP.3	Informally assess the degree of visual overlap of two numerical data distributions with similar variabilities, measuring the difference between the centers by expressing it as a multiple of a measure of variability. *For example, the mean height of players on the basketball team is 10 cm greater than the mean height of players on the soccer team, about twice the variability (mean absolute deviation) on either team; on a dot plot, the separation between the two distributions of heights is noticeable.*	51	2, 16, 17, 27, 36, 37, 47, 62	30	52
7.SP.4	Use measures of center and measures of variability for numerical data from random samples to draw informal comparative inferences about two populations. *For example, decide whether the words in a chapter of a seventh-grade science book are generally longer than the words in a chapter of a fourth-grade science book.*	52	5, 13, 25, 35, 40, 55, 67, 69	28	56

Standard	Descriptor	Pretest	Lessons	Practice Test A	Practice Test B
	Investigate chance processes and develop, use, and evaluate probability models.				
7.SP.5	Understand that the probability of a chance event is a number between 0 and 1 that expresses the likelihood of the event occurring. Larger numbers indicate greater likelihood. A probability near 0 indicates an unlikely event, a probability around $\frac{1}{2}$ indicates an event that is neither unlikely nor likely, and a probability near 1 indicates a likely event.	53	3, 7, 30, 32, 38, 54, 66	24	9
7.SP.6	Approximate the probability of a chance event by collecting data on the chance process that produces it and observing its long-run relative frequency, and predict the approximate relative frequency given the probability. *For example, when rolling a number cube 600 times, predict that a 3 or 6 would be rolled roughly 200 times, but probably not exactly 200 times.*	54	12, 21, 29, 31, 46, 51, 74	39	41
7.SP.7	Develop a probability model and use it to find probabilities of events. Compare probabilities from a model to observed frequencies; if the agreement is not good, explain possible sources of the discrepancy.				
7.SP.7.a	Develop a uniform probability model by assigning equal probability to all outcomes, and use the model to determine probabilities of events. *For example, if a student is selected at random from a class, find the probability that Jane will be selected and the probability that a girl will be selected.*	55	11, 20, 26, 33, 39, 56, 64	56	2
7.SP.7.b	Develop a probability model (which may not be uniform) by observing frequencies in data generated from a chance process. *For example, find the approximate probability that a spinning penny will land heads up or that a tossed paper cup will land open-end down. Do the outcomes for the spinning penny appear to be equally likely based on the observed frequencies?*	56	9, 23, 45, 53, 58, 71, 72	55	28
7.SP.8	Find probabilities of compound events using organized lists, tables, tree diagrams, and simulation.				
7.SP.8.a	Understand that, just as with simple events, the probability of a compound event is the fraction of outcomes in the sample space for which the compound event occurs.	57, 59	15, 19, 49, 52, 60, 61, 73	23	15, 16

Correlation Chart
Higher Scores on Math, Grade 7

Standard	Descriptor	Pretest	Lessons		Te
7.SP.8.b	Represent sample spaces for compound events using methods such as organized lists, tables, and tree diagrams. *For an event described in everyday language (e.g., "rolling double sixes"), identify the outcomes in the sample space which compose the event.*	5 8	4, 6, 34, 41, 43, 65	6, 52	
7.SP.8.c	Design and use a simulation to generate frequencies for compound events. *For example, use random digits as a simulation tool to approximate the answer to the question: If 40% of donors have type A blood, what is the probability that it will take at least 4 donors to find one with type A blood?*	60	18, 70	42	18

Correlation Chart
Higher Scores on Math, Grade 7

rawford _____ Date _____

a question and choose the best answer. Use the answer sheet provided at the end of
our answers. If the correct answer is not available, mark the letter for "Not Here."

1. The table shows the price of grapes.

Number of Pounds	3	4	7
Price	$11.94	$15.92	$27.86

Which equation gives the total cost y for x pounds of grapes?

(A) $y = 3.98x$

B $y = 8.94x$

C $y = 9.92x$

D $y = 20.86x$

$3\overline{)11.94}$
03.98
-9
29
27
-24
24
0

2. Tom's salary is $4,250.00 per month plus a commission of 5% of his monthly sales. Tom's sales this month are $10,250.00. What is his total income for this month?

F $9,375.00

(G) $4,762.50

H $10,462.50

J $31,500.00

$10,250$
$\times\ .05$
512.50

$4,250$
$+\ 512.5$
4762.5

3. Tamika runs at a rate of 1.5 miles every half hour. What is her unit rate?

A 1.0 mi/h

B 1.5 mi/h

(C) 3.0 mi/h

D 3.5 mi/h

4. Two milk cartons are leaking. Carton A leaks at a rate of $\frac{3}{4}$ quart every 15 minutes. Carton B leaks at a rate of $\frac{2}{3}$ quart every 20 minutes. Which statement is correct?

$B\ \frac{2}{3}\cdot\frac{3}{1}=\frac{6}{3}=2$

F The leak rate for Carton B is 3 qt/h.

$A\ \frac{3}{4}\cdot\frac{4}{1}=\frac{12}{4}$

G Carton B leaks faster than Carton A.

(H) Carton A leaks faster than Carton B.

J The leak rate for Carton A is 2 qt/h.

5. Lisa is buying a car that costs $16,520.00. She makes a down payment of $3,000.00. She takes out a 60-month loan for the remainder. If the rate of interest on the loan is 3.5%, how much is each of her monthly payments?

A $233.22

B $314.70

C $323.51

(D) $757.16

$16,520$
$-\ 3,000$
$13,520$

$13,520$
$\times\ .035$
67600
$+400600$
468200

$60\overline{)468.8200}$
-420
482
-480
200

6. What is the constant of proportionality shown in the graph?

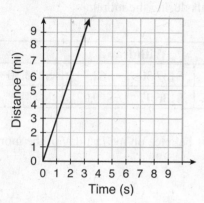

F $\frac{1}{3}$

G 1.5

H 3

J 6

7. Look at the information in the table.

Cups of Flour	2	3	3.5	4.25
Dozens of Donuts	6	9	10.5	13.75

Choose the statement that best describes the information in the table.

A The chart shows a proportional relationship with a constant of 3.

B The chart shows a proportional relationship with a constant of 2.

C The chart does not show a proportional relationship.

D Not Here

8. It takes Miguel 2 hours to drive 120 miles and 3 hours to drive 180 miles. Which equation gives the number of miles y for x hours?

F $y = 60x$

G $y = \frac{1}{60}x$

H $y = 3x$

J $y = (2 + 3)x$

9. Which graph does NOT show a proportional relationship?

A
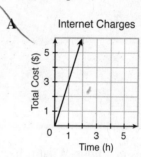
$6 per h

B
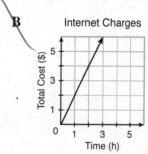
$6 per 3h

C
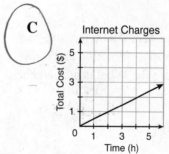

D
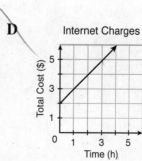
$2 per h

10. What is the unit rate shown in the graph?

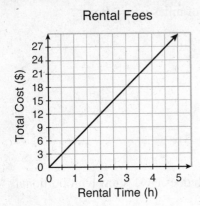

Rental Fees

F 3

G 6

H 9

J 12

11. Maria reads $15\frac{1}{2}$ pages in $\frac{1}{2}$ hour. What is her unit rate for reading?

A 7.75 pages per hour

B 15 pages per hour

C 16 pages per hour

D 31 pages per hour

12. Roland's income was $33,650.00 the first year on his job. He received a promotion and now earns $40,250.00 per year. What is his percent increase?

F 16.39%

G 19.61%

H 83.60%

J 119.61%

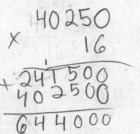

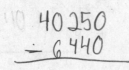

13. Misha has $1,052.50 in his bank account on the first of the month. He makes the following withdrawals during the month.

Withdrawals			
$300.00	$157.50	$62.73	$225.50
$100.08	$136.77	$69.92	

What is his balance on the last day of the month?

A $0

B $0.99

C $3.50

D $10.00

14. The March sales for the Widget Company were $20,625.57. April sales were $15,862.25. What is the net gain in sales from March to April?

F −$36,487.82

G −$4,763.32

H $4,763.32

J $36,487.82

15. Find x in lowest terms in the equation $x = \dfrac{-\frac{2}{7}}{-\frac{7}{8}}$.

A $x = \dfrac{16}{49}$

B $x = \dfrac{1}{4}$

C $x = -\dfrac{16}{49}$

D $x = -\dfrac{2}{8}$

16. The temperature at 10:00 P.M. is 32°F. It drops 3°F in each of 4 hours. What is the temperature at the end of the 4 hours?

F −20°F

G −12°F

H 7°F

J 20°F

17. Roy is baking bread. The recipe calls for $3\frac{1}{3}$ cups of flour. He wants to cut the recipe in half. How much flour does he need?

A 0.15 cup

B 1 cup

C 1.333333… cups

D 1.6666… cups

18. A school employee is putting up a flagpole. The top of the flagpole is 20 feet above the ground. Six feet of the flagpole is put into the ground. How long is the flagpole before it is put into the ground?

F −26 feet

G 14 feet

H 26 feet

J Not Here

19. In a football game, the home team has a gain of 4 yards, a loss of 3 yards, a gain of 2 yards, and a gain of 5 yards. What is the total loss or gain?

A 8-yard gain

B 8-yard loss

C 4-yard gain

D 4-yard loss

20. What is $6\frac{7}{12}$ as a decimal?

F 6.083333…

G 6.5

H 6.583333…

J 6.71

21. Mr. Martínez has a piece of pipe that is $42\frac{1}{2}$ inches long. He cuts the pipe into 5 equal pieces. How long is each piece?

A $4\frac{2}{5}$ inches

B $4\frac{1}{2}$ inches

C $8\frac{2}{5}$ inches

D $8\frac{1}{2}$ inches

22. The temperature dropped 50 degrees in 1 week. Which equation would you use to find the average change (y) in temperature per day?

F $y = -50 \div 7$

G $y = 50 \div 7$

H $y = -50 \div 1$

J $y = -50 \div 5$

23. The table gives the net gain and loss during a series of plays in a football game.

Gain/Loss							
0	4	−3	−4	2	10	−5	3

What is the average gain or loss rounded to the nearest tenth?

A   −0.9

B   −1.0

C   0.9

D   1.0

24. Mary has $300.00 in her savings account. In one month, she makes 5 withdrawals of $15.00 each and 2 deposits of $20.00 each. What is her new balance?

F $245.00

G $265.00

H $335.00

J   Not Here

25. Let s represent the price of a meal in the local coffee shop. Diana leaves a tip of 15%. Which expression represents the total amount Diana pays?

A $1.15s$

B s

C $15s$

D $s + 15$

26. The school sells plants as a fundraiser. At the end of the season, the price of each plant is reduced by 30%. If the original price is $25.00 per plant, what is the sale price?

F $5.50

G $7.50

H $17.50

J $24.50

27. Kim is hanging a picture and wants to center it between two window frames. The picture is 24.75 cm long. The distance between the window frames is 56.5 cm. How far from either window frame should she put the edge of the picture?

A   10.58 cm

B   15.75 cm

C   15.875 cm

D   18.625 cm

28. Mr. Bernal's camp group has 25 campers. The camp director tells him the group will increase to 35 campers. Which equation can be used to find the percent of increase?

F $25 + x = 35$

G $25 = 35x$

H $25 + 25x = 35$

J $35 - 25x = x$

29. Tyler has \$125.00 to spend on books and CDs. He buys one book for \$30.00. He wants to spend the rest on CDs that are on sale for \$9.00 each. Which of these statements is true?

A He can't buy any CDs.

B He can buy 11 CDs.

C He can buy more than 11 CDs.

D He can buy 10 CDs.

30. Simplify this expression:
$(3.5x + 23.7) + (16.5x - 14.3)$

F $20x + 9.4$

G $20x + 38$

H $17.2x + 2.2$

J $13.5x - 9.4$

31. Sophia sells makeup brushes for b dollars. For her holiday sale, she marks them down by 25%. Which expression represents the sale price?

A $1.25b$

B $1.75b$

C $0.25b$

D Not Here

32. A company moving to town promises the city government that it will increase the number of employees (e) by at least 15% in 5 years. It currently employs 4,525 people. What is the least number it will employ after 5 years?

F $e \geq 3,846$

G $e \geq 5,204$

H $e \geq 4,909$

J $e \geq 6,787$

33. Solve for x in $-\frac{8x}{33} = 5$.

A $x = -34.0$

B $x = -20.625$

C $x = 20.625$

D $x = 52.8$

34. Deepak solved the inequality $-\frac{x}{36} > 23$. His teacher told him that his solution of $x > -828$ was not correct. What did he do wrong?

F He should have changed the $>$ to $\geq$.

G He should have changed the $>$ to $\leq$.

H He should have changed the $>$ to $=$.

J He should have changed the $>$ to $<$.

35. The cost of taking a suitcase on an airplane is $25.00 for the first 50 pounds and $2.00 for each additional pound. Felix pays $66.00 for his suitcase. About how much does it weigh?

   A 52 pounds

   B 71 pounds

   C 79 pounds

   D 83 pounds

36. The seventh grade class sells magazine subscriptions as a fundraiser. Magazine A is $12.50 per year. Magazine B is $15.00 per year. The class profit is 15% of the sales. Which expression represents the class profit?

   F $0.15(12.50a + 15b)$

   G $0.15(27.50)$

   H $15(12.50a + 15b)$

   J $12.50a + 15b$

37. The distance between Philadelphia and Pittsburg is 305 miles. If the scale on a map is $\frac{1}{4}$ inch to 50 miles, about how far is it between these cities on the map?

   A 1.5 in.

   B 6.1 in.

   C 12.5 in.

   D 24.4 in.

38. The measurements of $\triangle ABC$ are: $AB = 3$, $BC = 4$, angle $B = 90°$.

Which triangle can you draw with these measurements?

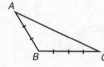 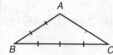

39. A plane intersects a sphere. What is the shape of the cross section?

   A triangle

   B square

   C parallelogram

   D circle

40. What is the formula for the area (A) of a circle?

   F $A = \pi d$

   G $A = \pi r^2$

   H $A = 2\pi r$

   J $A = 2\pi r^2$

41. What is the measure of ∠*DFE*?

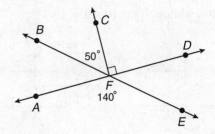

A 40°

B 50°

C 90°

D 140°

42. What is the surface area of the pyramid?

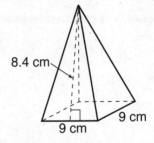

8.4 cm

9 cm

9 cm

F 151.2 cm²

G 232.2 cm²

H 302.4 cm²

J 378 cm²

43. Terry draws this diagram of his living and dining rooms.

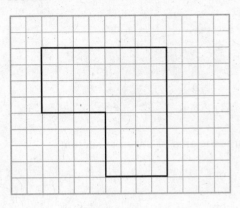

☐ = 1 cm

How many square meters of carpeting does Terry need to cover the entire floor if the scale used in the drawing is 1 cm:3 m?

A 48 m²

B 64 m²

C 432 m²

D 576 m²

44. The angles of a triangle are 30°, 60°, and 90°. Which best describes the number of triangles that can be drawn?

F no triangles

G one unique triangle

H two triangles

J many triangles

45. A rectangular prism is intersected by a plane.

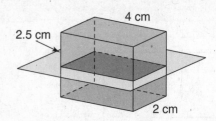

What is the area of the cross section?

A   4 cm²

B   5 cm²

C   8 cm²

D   10 cm²

46. What are the area (*A*) and circumference (*C*) of a circle with a radius of 3.5 inches?

F $C = 3.5\pi$ and $A = 12.25\pi$

G $C = 7\pi$ and $A = 12.25\pi$

H $C = 7\pi$ and $A = 3.5\pi$

J $C = 12.25\pi$ and $A = 7\pi$

47. Which two angles are NOT complementary?

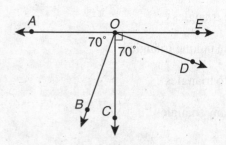

A $\angle AOB$ and $\angle BOC$

B $\angle AOB$ and $\angle BOE$

C $\angle BOC$ and $\angle COD$

D $\angle COD$ and $\angle DOE$

48. Tyrone is going to paint the walls and ceilings of his apartment. He draws pictures of the four rooms, although not to scale.

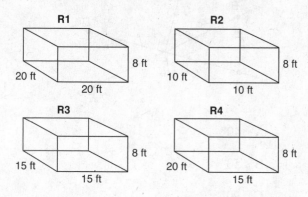

What is the minimum number of gallons of paint Tyrone must buy if 1 gallon covers 400 square feet and he doesn't deduct for door openings and windows?

F   6 gallons

G   8 gallons

H   14 gallons

J   Not Here

49. A political party wants to know if the environment is a major issue with the voters. Which sample will give the best results?

A   the members of the party conducting the survey

B   students on college campuses

C   a random sample of voters spread across the 50 states

D   a random sample of voters from one or two states

50. A random sample of a shipment of computers shows that 3 out of 75 computers are packed without a power cord. Which proportion should you use to find the number of computers in a shipment of 1,000 that will not contain a power cord?

F $\dfrac{3}{75} = \dfrac{1,000}{x}$

G $\dfrac{3}{75} = \dfrac{x}{1,000}$

H $\dfrac{75}{100} = \dfrac{x}{3}$

J $\dfrac{x}{75} = \dfrac{2}{1,000}$

51. Ana collects data on how many candy bars ten students in her class sold for the fundraiser. The amounts are shown in the table.

Candy Bars Sold
15, 10, 10, 5, 12, 20, 15, 5, 10, 10

What are the mean and MAD for these data?

A Mean = 3.44, and MAD = 11.2.

B Mean = 3.44, and MAD = 3.44.

C Mean = 10.0, and MAD = 1.2.

D Mean = 11.2, and MAD = 3.44.

52. Mrs. Saenz wants to know if the words are longer in the old seventh grade history book or in the new seventh grade history book. She has her students find the average length of the words in each book by taking a random sample from each book.

Old History Book
4, 8, 6, 3, 5, 4, 2, 7, 5, 9, 3, 4

New History Book
6, 5, 4, 7, 5, 6, 6, 3, 4, 5, 3, 6

What is the next thing Mrs. Saenz must do to get her results?

F Find the mean of each list.

G Find the MAD of each list.

H Take more word samples from each book.

J Compare the counts for the old history book with the counts for the new history book.

53. A jar contains 3 red jelly beans, 15 green jelly beans, and 2 yellow jelly beans. What is the best statement of the probability of picking a green jelly bean at random?

A The probability is 0.

B The probability is $\dfrac{1}{2}$.

C The probability is 1.

D The probability is close to 1.

54. You have a spinner like the one shown.

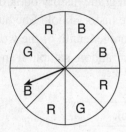

How often can you expect to land on a *B* in 500 spins?

F 125 times

G 188 times

H 300 times

J 500 times

55. You have a spinner like the one shown.

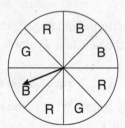

What is the complement of the probability that you will land on a *B* in one spin?

A $\frac{3}{8}$

B $\frac{2}{5}$

C $\frac{3}{5}$

D $\frac{5}{8}$

56. Jon draws a marble from a box. He records the color and then puts the marble back in the box. He does this several times and records the results in a table.

Color	Frequency
Clear	8
Red	12
Black	6
Green	15
Blue	11

What is the experimental probability of choosing a clear marble?

F $\frac{2}{13}$

G $\frac{3}{26}$

H $\frac{3}{13}$

J $\frac{11}{52}$

57. A drawer contains 8 pairs of black socks, 9 pairs of white socks, and 3 pairs of blue socks. What is the probability of choosing either a black pair or a white pair at random?

A $\frac{8}{17}$

B $\frac{8}{20}$

C $\frac{9}{20}$

D $\frac{17}{20}$

58. Billy tosses two number cubes and writes the products of the two numbers in a chart.

	1	2	3	4	5	6
1	1	2	3	4	5	6
2	2	4	6	8	10	12
3	3	6	9	12	15	18
4	4	8	12	16	20	24
5	5	10	15	20	25	30
6	6	12	18	24	30	36

What is the probability that the product will be less than 20?

F $\frac{31}{36}$

G $\frac{7}{9}$

H $\frac{1}{18}$

J $\frac{7}{36}$

59. A box contains 6 green balls, 8 red balls, 4 blue balls, and 1 black ball. What is the probability of choosing either a green, red, or black ball at random?

A $\frac{6}{19}$

B $\frac{9}{19}$

C $\frac{13}{19}$

D $\frac{15}{19}$

60. Anthony is developing a probability simulation and has created this table. He determines that the number 1 will measure his outcome.

Trial	Random Numbers	Outcome
1	1 3 1 5 6	2
2	9 1 1 3 0	2
3	3 0 6 5 1	1
4	1 2 0 8 8	1
5	9 4 3 3 4	0
6	2 1 0 3 8	1
7	4 0 9 2 8	0
8	0 7 8 1 6	1
9	0 7 1 5 2	1
10	8 2 5 8 5	0

What is the experimental probability of getting at least one 1 in a trial?

F $\frac{7}{10}$

G $\frac{9}{50}$

H $\frac{9}{10}$

J $\frac{7}{50}$

Name _____ Date _____

Ratios and Proportional Relationships

Modeled Instruction

DIRECTIONS: Read each question and choose the best answer. Use the answer sheet provided at the end of the workbook to record your answers. If the correct answer is not available, mark the letter for "Not Here."

1. An elevator moves at a constant speed of 32 feet per second. If this proportional relationship is shown on a coordinate graph, which point will NOT fall on the graph?

   A (1, 32)

   B (2, 64)

   C (3, 92)

   D (4, 128)

    Hint

   Multiply the first number in each ordered pair by 32 to find the second number.

2. Miguel paints $\frac{1}{4}$ of a room in 20 minutes. How much of a room does he paint per hour?

   F $\frac{1}{16}$

   G $\frac{3}{4}$

   H 1

   J 3

    Hint

   Write 20 minutes as a fraction of an hour. Then divide $\frac{1}{4}$ by that fraction.

3. The table shows a proportional relationship.

Time (h)	1	2	3	4	5
Distance (mi)	60	120	x	240	300

   What proportion would you use to find x?

   A $\frac{60}{1} = \frac{3}{x}$

   B $\frac{60}{3} = \frac{x}{1}$

   C $\frac{1}{60} = \frac{x}{3}$

   D $\frac{1}{60} = \frac{3}{x}$

    Hint

   Each ratio of the proportion should have time over distance.

4. Look at the graph.

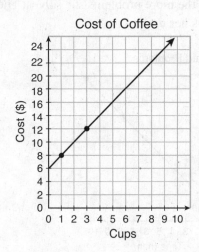

Cost of Coffee

Why does this graph NOT show a proportional relationship?

F The scale on the *x*-axis does not equal the scale on the *y*-axis.

G The line in the graph does not go through the point (1, 1).

H The line in the graph does not go through the point (0, 0).

J The values of *y* should decrease as the values of *x* increase.

Hint

What point must all graphs go through when they show a proportional relationship?

5. In a seventh grade class, the ratio of boys to girls is $\frac{3}{9}$. There are 28 students in the class. Which equation shows how to find the number of boys?

A $8b = 84$

B $3b = 77$

C $4b = 25$

D $12b = 84$

Hint

Set up a proportion of boys to students and cross multiply to find the equation.

6. An Internet café has a rate of $0.05 per minute of access. How would you find the unit rate per hour?

F Divide 1 by 0.05.

G Multiply 1 by 0.05.

H Divide 60 by 0.05.

J Multiply 0.05 by 60.

Hint

Determine the number of minutes in one hour and multiply by the rate.

Name _____ Date _____

7. The table shows the number of servings in a quart of ice cream.

Quarts	1	2	4	7
Servings	5	10	20	35

Which equation gives the number of servings in x quarts?

A $y = \dfrac{x}{5}$ **C** $y = x + 5$

B $y = 5x$ **D** $y = 20 - x$

Hint

Find the relationship between the numbers in the top row and the numbers in the bottom row.

8. The tables show the number of pages read by students over a four-week period. Which table does NOT show a proportional relationship?

F

Time (w)	1	2	3	4
Pages	12	24	36	48

G

Time (w)	1	2	3	4
Pages	15	30	48	60

H

Time (w)	1	2	3	4
Pages	7	14	21	28

J

Time (w)	1	2	3	4
Pages	8	16	24	32

Hint

Find the table in which the ratio of time to pages is not the same for all numbers.

9. The more time Sylvia spends on her math homework, the more problems she solves. The graph shows her progress.

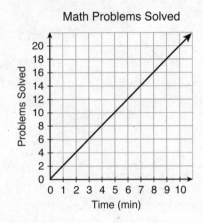

What is the unit rate?

A 1 **B** 2 **C** 3 **D** 4

Hint

The unit rate is the rate for 1 minute. Find 1 on the x-axis and determine the value of y.

10. A square yard of carpet costs $17.50. If a table were to show the number of square yards and the total cost of the carpet, which statement is true?

F The ratio of the total cost to the amount of carpet is always 17.50.

G The ratio of the amount of carpet to the total cost is always 17.50.

H The total cost is always 17.50 greater than the amount of carpet.

J The amount of carpet is always 17.50 times the total cost.

Hint

17.50 is the constant of proportionality.

11. Solve for x.

$$\frac{45x}{15} = 25$$

A 0.222…

B 0.8333…

C 0.888…

D 8.333…

Hint

First multiply both sides of the equation by 15. Then divide both sides by the number in front of the variable.

12. Single tires cost $58.75 each. During the spring sale, four tires cost $200.00. What is the percent of savings if you buy four tires, rounded to the nearest tenth?

F 14.9%

G 17.5%

H 82.5%

J 85.1%

Hint

Find the cost of four tires at the single-tire price. Find the percent of the amount saved at that price.

13. Find the quotient.

$$\frac{\frac{5}{8}}{\frac{3}{7}}$$

A $\frac{15}{56}$

B $\frac{35}{24}$

C $\frac{8}{15}$

D 2

Hint

Rewrite the compound fraction as a division problem and follow the rules for division of fractions.

14. Two pools are being filled with water. Pool A is filled at a rate of 3 gallons every $\frac{1}{2}$ hour. Pool B is filled at a rate of 4 gallons every $\frac{1}{4}$ hour. Which expression is correct for the pool that is filling faster?

F $\frac{3}{\frac{1}{2}}$

G $3 \times \frac{1}{2}$

H $\frac{4}{\frac{1}{4}}$

J $3 \div 4$

Hint

Set up ratios to find which pool is filling faster. The ratio you used for the faster pool will be your answer.

15. Simplify the fraction.

$$\frac{\frac{3}{8}}{\frac{2}{3}}$$

A $\frac{1}{5}$

B $\frac{3}{12}$

C $\frac{5}{11}$

D $\frac{9}{16}$

Hint

Write the complex fraction as a division problem and then follow the rule for division of fractions.

16. Peter makes $10.00 per hour as a server. The restaurant also gives him 15% of his wages as a bonus for good service. He works 40 hours this week. What are his total earnings for the week?

F $46.00

G $460.00

H $600.00

J Not Here

Hint

Multiply his wage by 1.15 and then by 40.

17. Look at the data in this table.

Time (s)	2	3	4	5
Distance (ft)	12	18	24	30

Which of the following is true?

A Constant of proportionality = 2; unit rate = 12.

B Constant of proportionality = 4; unit rate = 24.

C Constant of proportionality = 5; unit rate = 5.

D Constant of proportionality = 6; unit rate = 6.

Hint

Find the distance for 1 second.

18. An equation for a proportional relationship is $y = 4x$. Which of the following points would fall on the graph of this relationship?

F (1, 4), (3, 12), (4, 16), (6, 28)

G (1, 4), (3, 12), (4, 16), (6, 24)

H (3, 15), (4, 20), (5, 25), (6, 30)

J (0, 0), (1, 4), (2, 9), (3, 12)

Hint

Look for those points that have a constant of proportionality of 4.

19. Which of the following explains why a change in price from $30.00 to $15.00 is a 50% discount, but a change in price from $15.00 to $30.00 is a 100% increase?

A The assumption in the problem is wrong. It should be 50% in both cases.

B The assumption is wrong. It should be 100% in both cases.

C The assumption is wrong. It should be a 100% discount and a 50% increase.

D The difference is 15 in each case. The 15 is 100% when you start at 15. The 15 is 50% when you start at 30.

Hint

Find 50% of 30 and subtract it from 30. Find 100% of 15 and add it to 15.

20. Look at the table.

Quantity	4	8	9	16
Cost ($)	15	30	33.75	60

Which is the correct equation for this relationship?

F $y = 60x$

G $y = 240x$

H $y = 3.75x$

J $y = 9x$

Hint

Divide each bottom number by its top number and compare the results.

21. Which of these graphs does NOT show a proportional relationship?

A
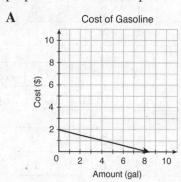

B
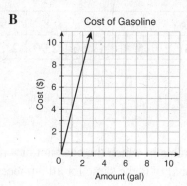

C
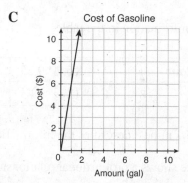

D
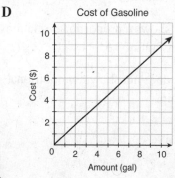

Hint

Three of the graphs go through one point that is necessary to have in a proportional relationship.

22. Which table shows a proportional relationship?

F

Gallons	1	2	3	4
Cost ($)	3	6	9	13

G

Gallons	3	7	9	12
Cost ($)	6.90	16.10	20.70	27.60

H

Gallons	1	2	3	4
Cost ($)	4	6	9	13

J

Gallons	6	7	8	9
Cost ($)	15.10	17.60	2.90	22.25

 Hint

Find the table in which the constant of proportionality is the same for all numbers.

23. Look at the information in the table.

Cups of Flour	4	7	8.5	9.25	10
Cookies (dz)	8	14	17	18.5	20

Which statement best describes the information?

A The table shows a proportional relationship with a constant of 5.

B The table shows a proportional relationship with a constant of 3.5.

C The table does not show a proportional relationship.

D Not Here

 Hint

Divide each number in the bottom row by the number in the top row to find the constant of proportionality.

24. Look at the graph.

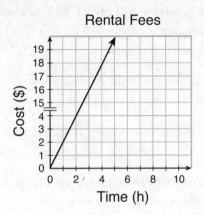

Rental Fees

What is the constant of proportionality shown in the graph?

F 1   **H** 2

G 1.5   **J** 2.5

 Hint

Find the value of *y* when the value of *x* = 1.

25. A cellular phone sells for $99.00. The company is offering a discount of 33% for a one-year service contract. There is 8.25% sales tax. How much will Bert have to pay for the phone if he takes the one-year service contract?

A $35.36

B $40.83

C $71.80

D $73.50

 Hint

Find the price of the phone after the discount and then add the tax to that price.

Ratios and Proportional Relationships

Independent Practice

DIRECTIONS: Read each question and choose the best answer. Use the answer sheet provided at the end of the workbook to record your answers. If the correct answer is not available, mark the letter for "Not Here."

26. Look at the graph.

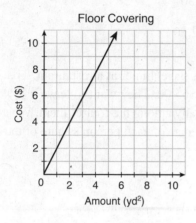

Which of the following is NOT a true statement?

F The unit rate is 2.

G The constant of proportionality is 2.

H The point (3, 6) is in the proportional relationship.

J The point (5, 8) is in the proportional relationship.

27. At the class car wash, the students wash 16 cars in 2 hours. What is their unit rate?

A 4 cars per hour

B 8 cars per hour

C 16 cars per hour

D 32 cars per hour

28. Look at the graph.

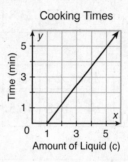

Why does the graph NOT show a proportional relationship?

F The values of y should decrease as the values of x increase.

G The line in the graph does not go through the point (1, 1).

H The scale on the x-axis does not match the scale on the y-axis.

J The line in the graph does not go through the point (0, 0).

29. Which table shows a proportional relationship?

A

Days	1	2	3	4
Time Doing Homework (min)	3.25	6.50	9.75	13

B

Days	1	2	3	4
Time Doing Homework (min)	7.6	15.2	23.8	31.6

C

Days	1	2	3	4
Time Doing Homework (min)	5.4	10.8	16.5	24.7

D

Days	1	2	3	4
Time Doing Homework (min)	8	16	24	36

30. Which of these sets of ordered pairs does NOT form a proportional relationship?

F (0,0), (1, 3), (2, 6), (3, 9)

G (0,0), (2, 4), (3, 6), (4, 8)

H (0,0), (1, 5), (2, 6), (3, 8)

J (0,0), (1, 5), (2, 10), (3, 15)

31. Sara walks $\frac{1}{2}$ mile every 20 minutes. How do you find her unit rate per hour?

A Multiply $\frac{1}{2}$ by 20.

B Divide $\frac{1}{2}$ by 20.

C Multiply $\frac{1}{2}$ by $\frac{1}{3}$.

D Divide $\frac{1}{2}$ by $\frac{1}{3}$.

32. Trevor gets paid $1,250.00 per month, plus a commission of 5% of his monthly sales. His sales at the end of this month are $10,350.00. How much is his total pay for the month?

F $580.00

G $1,312.50

H $1,767.50

J $10,412.50

33. Four friends have dinner at a restaurant. The total bill is $65.00. They want to leave a 15% tip divided equally among the four of them. What is the best estimate of each person's share of the tip?

A $2.00

B $2.50

C $3.00

D $3.25

34. Nicolás is riding his bicycle to raise money for his favorite charity. He rides $7\frac{3}{4}$ miles every $\frac{1}{2}$ hour. The table shows how far he rides in given times.

Distance (mi)	$7\frac{3}{4}$	w	x	y	z
Time (h)	$\frac{1}{2}$	1	$1\frac{1}{2}$	2	$2\frac{1}{2}$

What are the values of w, x, y, and z?

F $w = 15\frac{1}{2}$, $x = 23\frac{3}{4}$, $y = 31\frac{1}{2}$, $z = 37\frac{1}{2}$

G $w = 15\frac{1}{2}$, $x = 23\frac{1}{4}$, $y = 31$, $z = 38\frac{3}{4}$

H $w = 15\frac{3}{4}$, $x = 23\frac{1}{4}$, $y = 31$, $z = 38\frac{3}{4}$

J $w = 15\frac{3}{4}$, $x = 23\frac{1}{4}$, $y = 31\frac{1}{2}$, $z = 37\frac{1}{2}$

Name _____   Date _____

35. Look at the graph.

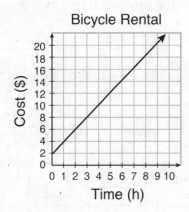

Bicycle Rental

Which of the following is true?

A The graph does not show a proportional relationship because the *x*-scale and *y*-scale are not the same.

B The graph does not show a proportional relationship because it does not go through the point (0, 0).

C The graph shows a proportional relationship.

D The line connecting these points will go through the point (0, 0).

36. Three pounds of tomatoes cost $8.07, 4 pounds cost $10.76, and 6 pounds cost $16.14. Which equation gives the total cost *y* of *x* pounds of tomatoes?

F $x = 2.69y$

G $y = 3.04x$

H $y = 2.69x$

J $x = 3.04y$

37. The table below shows a proportional relationship.

Time (min)	3	8	10	15
Distance (mi)	7	$18\frac{2}{3}$	$23\frac{1}{3}$	x

What is the value of *x*?

A $x = 35$

B $x = 33\frac{3}{7}$

C $x = 41\frac{2}{7}$

D $x = 28\frac{5}{8}$

38. In 2010, the school district employed 525 teachers. In 2011, the number of teachers was 480. What is the percent of increase or decrease?

F 8.57% increase

G 91.42% decrease

H 8.57% decrease

J 91.42% increase

39. Five kilograms of peaches cost $6.75. The cost of peaches is a proportional relationship. Maureen makes a graph that shows the number of kilograms and the total cost. Which of the following would NOT be true about the graph?

A The graph goes through the point (0, 0).

B The graph goes through the point (1, 1.35).

C The graph goes through the point (7, 9.45).

D The graph goes through the point (9, 11.15).

40. A swimmer swims $2\frac{1}{2}$ meters in $\frac{1}{2}$ minute. What is her unit rate?

   F $\frac{1}{5}$ m/min

   G $\frac{5}{4}$ m/min

   H   2 m/min

   J   5 m/min

41. Rashid's monthly salary is $4,250.00, plus a 2.5% commission on his monthly sales. If his sales for this month are $62,825.00, how much does he earn this month?

   A $5,312.50

   B $5,820.63

   C $5,926.87

   D $9,956.25

42. An airplane flies at a constant speed of 650 miles per hour. Carlos graphs this relationship on a coordinate plane. Which point lies on the graph?

   F   (2, 1200)

   G   (650, 0)

   H   (1, 650)

   J   (0, 650)

43. Which table shows the amount of money Kamal earns for washing windows if he earns the same amount for every window?

A

Number of Windows	1	3	5	7
Amount Earned ($)	1.50	4.25	7.25	10.25

B

Number of Windows	1	3	5	7
Amount Earned ($)	1.50	4.00	7.25	9.75

C

Number of Windows	1	3	5	7
Amount Earned ($)	1.50	4.50	7.50	10.50

D

Number of Windows	1	3	5	7
Amount Earned ($)	1.50	4.50	7.75	10.50

44. An equation for the cost of x pounds of peppers is $y = 2.5x$. There is no discount for buying more than one pound. Which of the following is true?

   F   The cost for 3 pounds is $7.75.

   G   The cost for 4 pounds is $10.00.

   H   The cost for 5 pounds is $12.25.

   J   The cost for 8 pounds is $16.00.

45. Find the quotient.

$$\dfrac{3\frac{2}{3}}{1\frac{1}{2}}$$

  A   2   **C** $4\frac{1}{2}$

  B $2\frac{4}{9}$ **D** $5\frac{1}{2}$

46. Lenora jogs at the rate of 3 miles every $\frac{3}{5}$ hour. What is her unit rate?

  F $\frac{3}{15}$ mi/h

  G $1\frac{4}{5}$ mi/h

  H $3\frac{3}{5}$ mi/h

  J   5 mi/h

47. Look at the graph.

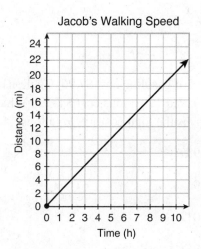

Jacob's Walking Speed

Which statement is true?

  A   Jacob walks 2 miles in 1 hour.

  B   Jacob walks 1 mile in 1 hour.

  C   Jacob walks $\frac{1}{2}$ mile in $\frac{1}{2}$ hour.

  D   Jacob walks $3\frac{1}{2}$ miles in 2 hours.

48. Which of these tables shows a proportional relationship?

F

Cars Washed	1	1.5	2	2.5
Time (h)	2	3	5	6

G

Cars Washed	1	1.5	2	2.5
Time (h)	3	4	6	8

H

Cars Washed	1	1.5	2	2.5
Time (h)	2	3	4	5

J

Cars Washed	1	1.5	2	2.5
Time (h)	3	4	6	7

49. Lemons cost $3.50 for one dozen. Two dozen lemons cost $6.30. Five dozen lemons cost $14.87. Which of the following is true?

  A   This is a proportional relationship.

  B   This is not a proportional relationship.

  C   The unit rate is $0.29.

  D   Four dozen lemons cost $14.00.

50. A bathtub fills at a constant rate. The amount of water in the bathtub increases by $\frac{3}{4}$ gallon every $\frac{1}{4}$ minute. What is the unit rate?

  F $\frac{3}{16}$ gal/min

  G $\frac{1}{3}$ gal/min

  H $1\frac{3}{4}$ gal/min

  J   3 gal/min

51. Look at the graph.

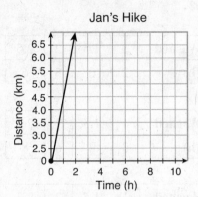

Jan's Hike

What constant of proportionality and unit rate are shown in the graph?

A Constant of proportionality = 3.5;
unit rate = 3.5.

B Constant of proportionality = 3.5;
unit rate = 1.

C Constant of proportionality = 1;
unit rate = 3.5.

D Constant of proportionality = 7;
unit rate = 7.

52. Look at this table of a proportional relationship.

Time (d)	1	2	3	4
Homework (h)	3.85	x	y	z

What are the values of x, y, and z?

F $x = 7.7$, $y = 11.25$, $z = 15.4$

G $x = 7.7$, $y = 11.25$, $z = 15.25$

H $x = 7.3$, $y = 11.25$, $z = 15.4$

J $x = 7.7$, $y = 11.55$, $z = 15.4$

53. Becker and his team clean houses. From Monday through Friday, they can clean 20 houses. If they clean the same number of houses each day, what is their unit rate?

A 3 houses per day

B 4 houses per day

C 5 houses per day

D 6 houses per day

54. Belinda types 2 pages in 3 minutes. If she types at a constant rate, which equation can be used to find p, the number of pages she can type in x minutes?

F $p = 3x$

G $p = \dfrac{2}{3}x$

H $p = \dfrac{1}{12}x$

J Not Here

55. Two gallons of gasoline cost $7.96, 5 gallons cost $19.90, and 12 gallons cost $47.76. Which equation gives the total cost y of x gallons?

A $y = 2.98x$

B $y = 3.96x$

C $y = 4.01x$

D $y = 3.98x$

56. The state usually charges 8.25% sales tax on clothes. During the tax-free weekend, no sales tax is charged. How much will Joseph save on a $60.00 purchase during the tax-free weekend?

F $0.50

G $4.95

H $49.50

J $55.05

57. A ship travels at a constant speed of 30 knots in 2 hours. The first officer is making a graph of this proportional relationship. Which of the following points will be on the graph?

A (0, 15)

B (15, 0)

C (1, 30)

D Not Here

58. Each roll of wallpaper is $17.95. A table shows the number of rolls and the total cost of the rolls. Which of the following is true about the data in the table if this is a proportional relationship?

F The ratio of the number of rolls to the total cost is 17.95.

G The ratio of the total cost to the number of rolls is 17.95.

H The number of rolls is always 17.95 times the total cost.

J The total cost is always 17.95 greater than the number of rolls.

59. The point (1, 18) appears on a coordinate graph of a proportional relationship. Which of the following is NOT true?

A The point (0, 0) is on the graph.

B The point (2, 36) is on the graph.

C The point (4, 72) is on the graph.

D The point (7, 128) is on the graph.

60. The equation $y = 3.48x$ is used to create a table of a proportional relationship. To which of the following situations does this apply?

F The supermarket has milk on sale: 2 gallons for $6.96.

G The local department store has shirts on sale: 3 shirts for $15.00.

H The grocery store has potatoes on sale: 4 pounds for $16.00.

J The local nursery has plants on sale: $2.98 each.

61. A file downloads from the Internet at a constant rate of 154 KB per second. Which of the following points will appear on a graph of this proportional relationship?

A (2, 300)

B (3, 462)

C (5, 700)

D (7, 1,000)

62. A snowstorm dumped 18 inches of snow in a 12-hour period. The snow fell at a constant rate. What is the unit rate per hour?

F 0.666… in./h

G 1.5 in./h

H 1.666… in./h

J 2.5 in./h

63. The graphs show the number of workbook pages several students completed in one four-day period. Which graph shows a proportional relationship?

A   Workbook Pages Completed

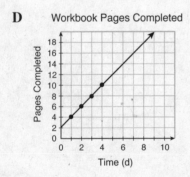

B   Workbook Pages Completed

C   Workbook Pages Completed

D   Workbook Pages Completed

64. Ms. Amaya spends 17 hours in a 2-week period grading papers. She grades papers at a constant rate.

Time (w)	2	3	4	5
Hours Grading Papers	17	x	y	z

What are the values of x, y, and z?

F $x = 25.5$, $y = 35$, $z = 43$

G $x = 26$, $y = 35$, $z = 43$

H $x = 25.5$, $y = 34$, $z = 42.5$

J $x = 25.5$, $y = 42.5$, $z = 59.5$

65. Look at the graph.

June's Babysitting

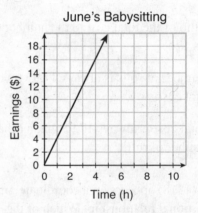

What constant of proportionality and what unit rate are shown in the graph?

A   0

B   2

C   4

D   6

66. In one survey, a candidate for school council president is expected to receive 80 votes, with a 5% margin of error. A second survey also shows the margin of error as 5%, but with 6 additional votes. What is the total number of votes she is expected to receive according to the second survey?

F 80

G 85

H 95

J 100

67. The teacher said it takes 20 minutes to write each test for his classes. He creates the following table.

Number of tests	1	2	3	4
Time (min)	20	40	60	80

Which of the following is NOT true for the data in the table?

A The table shows a proportional relationship.

B The unit rate per hour is 3.

C The table does not show a proportional relationship.

D The ratios are the same for all entries in the table.

68. Look at the data in the table.

Time (min)	1	3	5	8
Water Used (gal)	6	18	30	48

Which is the correct graph for the data in the table?

F
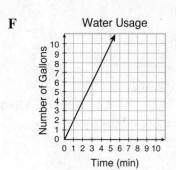

G
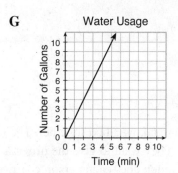

H
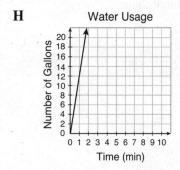

J
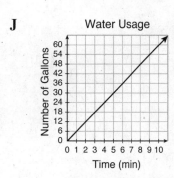

69. Roberta's yearly salary is $32,600.00. She also receives a commission of 2% on her sales over $100,000.00. Her yearly sales are $125,600.00. What is her yearly income?

   A $33,112.00

   B $33,252.00

   C $34,600.00

   D $35,112.00

70. Eight pounds of cashew nuts cost $12.00, 3 pounds cost $4.50, and 7 pounds cost $10.50. Which equation gives y, the total for x pounds of cashew nuts?

   F $y = 12x$

   G $y = 1.5x$

   H $y = 8x$

   J $y = .66x$

71. Three friends are taking a taxi together. The taxi fare is $25.80. They want to give the driver a 10% tip. How much does each person contribute to cover the total amount?

   A $7.74

   B $9.46

   C $28.38

   D Not Here

72. A water tank is leaking at a constant rate of 3 gallons in $\frac{1}{4}$ hour. Octavio graphs this proportional relationship on a coordinate graph. Which of the following points does NOT fall on his graph?

   F $(0, 0)$

   G $(1, 12)$

   H $(2, 20)$

   J $(3, 36)$

73. The sign below is on display in the rug department of a furniture store.

SALE! Prices reduced by x%	
Original Price	Sale Price
$1,000.00	$750.00
$1,500.00	$1,125.00
$2,000.00	$1,500.00

What is the value of x?

   A $x = 1.75$

   B $x = 16$

   C $x = 25$

   D $x = 75$

Name _____   Date _____

74. Look at the graph.

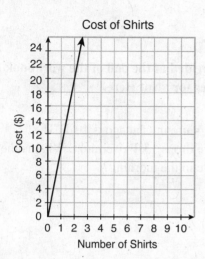

Cost of Shirts

Which equation represents the cost of shirts?

F $y = 20x$

G $y = 10x$

H $y = 2x$

J $y = x$

75. The table shows a proportional relationship.

Time (s)	4	7	9	12
Distance (mi)	11.6	20.3	26.1	x

What is the value of x?

A 5.8

B 8.7

C 34.8

D 36

The Number System

Modeled Instruction

Read each question and choose the best answer. Use the answer sheet provided at the end of the workbook to record your answers. If the correct answer is not available, mark the letter for "Not Here."

1. Kate has a piece of material that is $3\frac{3}{4}$ yards long. She needs 5 pieces of equal length. How long will each piece be if she uses all the material?

   A $\frac{3}{4}$ yard

   B $\frac{12}{20}$ yard

   C $1\frac{1}{3}$ yards

   D $1\frac{2}{3}$ yards

    Hint

   Divide the total number of yards by the number of pieces.

2. What is $5\frac{7}{8}$ as a decimal?

   F 5.375

   G 5.875

   H 6.142

   J 7.125

    Hint

   Change the mixed number to an improper fraction and divide the numerator by the denominator.

3. The temperature in Chicago is 10°F. The temperature drops 15°F overnight. What is the temperature in the morning?

   A −25°F

   B −5°F

   C 5°F

   D 25°F

    Hint

   A drop of 15° can be expressed as −15°.

4. Find the sum.

   $$24\frac{1}{3} + \left(-38\frac{2}{3}\right)$$

   F −63

   G $-14\frac{1}{3}$

   H $14\frac{1}{3}$

   J 63

    Hint

   Change the mixed numbers to improper fractions and perform the operation indicated by the symbols.

5. The first play in a football game starts at the 50-yard line and results in a gain of 25 yards for Team A. On the next play, Team B has a gain of 25 yards in the opposite direction. Where is the ball after the second play?

A twenty-five yards closer to the Team A goal post

B twenty-five yards on the other side of where it was at the beginning of the game

C where it was at the beginning of the game

D fifty yards on the other side of where it was at the beginning of the game

Hint

Make a diagram moving 25 units to the right and then 25 units to the left. See where you end up.

6. Ben's bread recipe calls for $3\frac{1}{4}$ cups of flour for a $1\frac{1}{2}$-pound loaf. How much flour will he need to bake a 3-pound loaf?

F $2\frac{5}{8}$ cups

G $4\frac{3}{4}$ cups

H $4\frac{7}{8}$ cups

J $6\frac{1}{2}$ cups

Hint

Since 3 is twice $1\frac{1}{2}$, multiply $3\frac{1}{4}$ by 2.

7. Lina is driving from Los Angeles to New York City, a distance of 2,750 miles. If she drives between 400 and 500 miles per day, what is the minimum number of days it will take her?

A $5\frac{1}{2}$ days

B $6\frac{1}{4}$ days

C 6.2 days

D 7 days

Hint

Since the question asks for the minimum number of days, divide the total distance by the maximum speed.

8. Heidi's strawberry pie recipe calls for 3 pounds of sugar and 7 pounds of strawberries. How many pounds of sugar are needed for 1 pound of strawberries?

F $\frac{3}{7}$ pound

G $2\frac{1}{3}$ pounds

H 4 pounds

J 10 pounds

Hint

The amount of strawberries is $\frac{1}{7}$, so find $\frac{1}{7}$ of the sugar.

9. Find the product.

$$-\frac{7}{8} \times -5\frac{2}{5}$$

A $-4\frac{29}{40}$

B $-2\frac{5}{8}$

C $2\frac{5}{8}$

D $4\frac{29}{40}$

Hint

Change the mixed number to an improper fraction and follow the rules for multiplication of fractions.

10. Alberto's company had sales of $2,846.00 during June and $5,280.00 in returns. What is the net gain in sales for the month?

F $-\$8,126.00$

G $-\$2,434.00$

H $\$2,434.00$

J $\$8,126.00$

Hint

Find the difference between the two numbers and then assign the appropriate sign.

11. An airplane starts in San Francisco and flies 2,571 miles to New York. It then flies 713 miles back to Chicago. How much farther must the plane fly to end up in San Francisco?

A 1,858 miles

B 2,868 miles

C 3,284 miles

D Not Here

Hint

Subtract the distance between New York and Chicago from the distance between San Francisco and New York.

12. The school has 3 seventh grade classes. Class 1 raises $614.33 for the class project, Class 2 raises $1,492.16, and Class 3 raises $1,276.00. Their expenses are $513.00. What is their profit?

F $2,666.83

G $2,869.49

H $3,382.49

J $3,895.49

Hint

Add the amounts raised and then subtract the expenses.

13. Steven has $1,294.00 in his savings account. He makes a deposit of $100.00 and for the next 4 weeks, he withdraws $350.50 each week. What is his balance at the end of the 4 weeks?

A −$108.00

B −$8.00

C $493.00

D $1,244.50

Hint

Add the deposit to the beginning balance and then subtract the four withdrawals.

14. Renaldo has a piece of wood that is 8 feet long. How many pieces $1\frac{1}{2}$ feet long can he cut from the wood?

F 5

G 6

H 7

J 12

Hint

Divide the total length by the length of each piece. Give your answer in whole pieces.

15. The table below shows Nicole's scores. What is her average score for six rounds?

Round	1	2	3	4	5	6
Score	4	−2	3	1	−1	2

A $-2\frac{1}{6}$

B $-1\frac{1}{6}$

C $1\frac{1}{6}$

D $2\frac{1}{6}$

Hint

Add the scores and then divide by the number of scores.

16. Solve for x.

$$x = -(3\frac{3}{8}) - (8\frac{3}{4})$$

F $x = -12\frac{1}{8}$

G $x = -11$

H $x = -6\frac{5}{8}$

J $x = 12\frac{1}{8}$

Hint

Rewrite the problem as the addition of two negative numbers and then find the sum.

17. A water tank loses 15 gallons of water through evaporation. A series of heavy rains adds 15 gallons to the tank. What is the overall increase or decrease of water in the tank?

A The tank remains 15 gallons short.

B The tank returns to the original level.

C The tank contains twice the amount of water it starts with.

D The tank contains half the amount of water it starts with.

 Hint

Add 15 to any number and then subtract 15 from the sum. Compare your answer to your original number.

18. A mountain climber climbed $\frac{1}{3}$ mile up a cliff and then rested. She did this 5 times. How far did she climb?

F 0.333… mile

G 0.666… mile

H $\frac{1}{13}$ mile

J $1\frac{2}{3}$ miles

 Hint

Multiply the individual distances by the number of times she climbed.

19. The price of stock in a software company rises $36.00 over a period of 20 days. On average, how much does it rise per day?

A $0.55

B $1.82

C $16.00

D Not Here

 Hint

To find the average, divide the total by the number of days.

20. The temperature in Denver is 35°C on Friday. Over the weekend, the temperature drops 30°C. What is the temperature on Monday morning?

F −65°C

G −5°C

H 5°C

J 65°C

 Hint

Subtract the weekend drop in temperature from the temperature on Friday.

21. Look at the table.

Fraction	$\frac{1}{4}$	$\frac{3}{8}$	$\frac{7}{12}$
Decimal Equivalent	x	y	z

Solve for x, y, and z.

A

x	y	z
0.5	0.375	0.58333…

B

x	y	z
0.25	0.37555…	0.58333…

C

x	y	z
0.25	0.375	0.58333…

D

x	y	z
0.5	0.37555…	0.58333…

Hint

To change a fraction to a decimal, divide the numerator by the denominator.

22. The main roof beam of a barn is 25 feet long. Twenty-two feet are inside the barn. Which is the correct equation to determine how many feet are outside the barn?

F $x = 25 - 22$

G $x = 25 + 22$

H $x = 22 - 3$

J $x = 22 + 3$

Hint

Subtract the amount inside the barn from the total.

23. The credit limit on Mark's credit card is $500.00. For every $100.00 his balance is over his limit, the bank charges him $5.00. If Mark's balance reaches $750.00, how much will the bank charge in transaction fees, if they prorate the fee?

A $2.50

B $5.00

C $12.50

D Not Here

Hint

Calculate the number of hundreds Mark is over his limit. Then calculate how many $5.00 charges the bank will add.

24. Is -15.25 a rational number? Why?

   F   Yes. It can be written as $15\frac{1}{2}$.

   G   No. It is less than 0.

   H   Yes. It can be written as $-15\frac{1}{4}$.

   J   No. When added to 15.25, the sum is 0.

Hint

A rational number can be written as a fraction.

25. José gets in an elevator on the first floor. He goes up 22 floors and then goes down 25 floors to the parking lot. Which equation shows the floor he is on when he leaves the elevator?

   A $1 + 22 - 25 = -2$

   B $1 + 25 - 22 = 3$

   C $1 - 25 + 22 = 2$

   D $1 + 22 - 25 = -3$

Hint

Think of "up" as a positive number and "down" as a negative number.

The Number System

Independent Practice

DIRECTIONS: Read each question and choose the best answer. Use the answer sheet provided at the end of the workbook to record your answers. If the correct answer is not available, mark the letter for "Not Here."

26. Which of the following is NOT true for the sum of $-5 + -8$?

    F   The sum will be a negative number.

    G   To find the sum, add the absolute values of the two addends and take the negative sign.

    H   The sum will be a positive number because both addends are negative.

    J   The sum is -13.

27. The seventh grade students are packing 150 boxes of books to send to children in poor countries. They have packed $\frac{2}{3}$ of the boxes. How many boxes are left to pack?

    A   50

    B   100

    C   150

    D   Not Here

28. If you convert $\frac{16}{24}$ to a decimal, which of the following is true?

    F   The decimal is 0.6.

    G   The decimal is 0.67.

    H   The decimal is 0.6667.

    J   The decimal has a digit that repeats.

29. Which of these is NOT true for the quotient of $-x \div y$?

    A   The quotient will be a positive number.

    B   The quotient will be a negative number.

    C   The quotient will be the same as the quotient in $x \div -y$.

    D   The quotient is the same as the quotient in $-(x \div y)$.

30. George has a recipe that calls for $3\frac{1}{4}$ cups of flour for every $1\frac{1}{4}$ cups of water. He accidentally adds $2\frac{1}{2}$ cups of water to the flour. How much additional flour must he add for the recipe to come out correctly?

    F $3\frac{1}{4}$ cups

    G   4 cups

    H $4\frac{1}{2}$ cups

    J $6\frac{1}{2}$ cups

31. Rosa has $432.50 in her checking account. She deposits $50.00 and then withdraws $25.46 two times. What is her balance?

    A $381.58

    B $431.58

    C $457.04

    D $482.50

32. Palak earned $2,156.00 during the first six months of the year. During the second six months, he lost $1,583.00. What is his net gain or loss?

   F   −$3,438.00

   G   −$573.00

   H $573.00

   J $3,438.00

33. Shanti has a piece of silk that is 4.55 meters long. She wants to cut it into five shorter pieces. What is the length of each piece?

   A   0.091 m

   B   0.91 m

   C   9.1 cm

   D   9 mm

34. Which of the following is true for the equation $x = -3,281 + 5,376$?

   F   The sum is a negative number.

   G   The sum is 2,095.

   H   The sum is 8,657.

   J   The sum is −2,095.

35. Write $\frac{4\frac{1}{2}}{250}$ as a decimal.

   A   0.012

   B   0.018

   C   12.00

   D   18.0

36. Which of the following is true for the equation $x = -3,254 + 8,628 + -5,642$?

   F $x = -268$

   G $x = 268$

   H $x = 6,240$

   J $x = 11,016$

37. Marion raised $1,332.18 for her favorite charity. Her expenses were $4.25. Jake raised $1,652.00 for his favorite charity. His expenses were $367.00. Who gave more to charity and by how much?

   A   Marion by $320.00

   B   Jake by $320.00

   C   Jake by $42.93

   D   Marion by $42.93

38. The temperature at a location in the Northern Hemisphere is 32°C. The temperature at a location in the Southern Hemisphere is 40°C cooler. What is the temperature in the Southern Hemisphere?

F −72°C

G −8°C

H 8°C

J 72°C

39. Mr. Ramos's mortgage is $62,426.50. His payment is $1,142.16 per month. He makes 3 payments and adds an additional $500.00 to the second payment. What is his mortgage balance?

A $57,500.02

B $58,500.02

C $59,500.02

D $61,284.34

40. Gold is selling for $1,758.33 per ounce one week. The next week it is selling for $1,523.47 per ounce. What is the net gain or loss?

F −$232.86

G $117.43

H $232.86

J Not Here

41. In one seventh grade class, 9 out of 27 students play in the school band. Write this number as a decimal.

A 0.3

B 0.33

C 0.333…

D 0.33444…

42. Which of the following is true for the expression $3\frac{2}{8} \times -5$?

F The product can be found by solving $-5(3 - \frac{2}{8})$ and will be positive.

G The product can be found by solving $-5(3 + \frac{2}{8})$ and will be positive.

H The product can be found by solving $2\frac{6}{8} \times 5$ and will be negative.

J The product can be found by solving $-5(\frac{2}{8} + 3)$.

43. Pat's recipe calls for $3\frac{2}{3}$ cups of milk. She quadruples the recipe. How much milk does she need?

A 12 cups

B $14\frac{2}{3}$ cups

C 15 cups

D $18\frac{2}{3}$ cups

44. The highest point on Earth is Mount Everest, which is 8,848 meters above sea level. The lowest point is the Dead Sea at 399 meters below sea level. How far apart are the highest and lowest points?

F   −9,247 m

G   −8,449 m

H   8,449 m

J   9,247 m

45. The table shows Fred's scores on a series of math tests. What is his average score?

Tests	1	2	3	4	5	6
Scores	87	71	92	63	84	99

A   82

B   82.66

C   82.666…

D   82.667

46. Hannah has 3 pizzas to divide among 7 people. If each pizza can be cut into 8 pieces, how much will each person receive?

F   0.428 piece

G   0.875 piece

H   3 pieces

J $3\frac{3}{7}$ pieces

47. Which of the following is NOT true for this expression: $3\frac{7}{8} \times -15.6$?

A   The product is the same as 3.875×15.6 and is negative.

B   The product is the same as $3\frac{7}{8} \times 15\frac{3}{5}$ and is positive.

C   The product is a negative number.

D   The product is the same as $60\frac{45}{100}$ and is negative.

48. Convert $1\frac{1}{2}$ and $\frac{1}{3}$ to decimals. Then look at the statements explaining why the two decimals are not the same. Choose the statement that is NOT true.

F   The decimal for $1\frac{1}{2}$ contains a 5, while the decimal for $\frac{1}{3}$ contains a 3.

G   The decimal for $\frac{1}{3}$ has a repeating digit, while the decimal for $1\frac{1}{2}$ does not.

H   The decimal for $1\frac{1}{2}$ contains a whole number, while the decimal for $\frac{1}{3}$ does not.

J   The decimal for $\frac{1}{3}$ is larger than the decimal for $1\frac{1}{2}$.

49. The highest temperature recorded on Earth is 134.1°F in Death Valley, California. The lowest temperature is −87°F recorded in North Ice, Greenland. What is the difference between these two temperatures?

A   −221.1°F

B   −47.1°F

C   47.1°F

D   221.1°F

50. The scale on a map shows $1\frac{1}{2}$ inches equals 50 miles. How many miles are represented by 3 inches?

F   25 mi

G   75 mi

H   100 mi

J   Not Here

51. Which of the following is an example of the rule about the sign of the quotient of two numbers?

A $-\left(\frac{x}{y}\right) = \frac{(-x)}{y} = \frac{x}{(-y)}$

B $-\left(\frac{x}{y}\right) = \frac{x}{y} = \frac{x}{(-y)}$

C $\left(\frac{x}{y}\right) = \frac{(-x)}{y} = \frac{x}{(-y)}$

D $-\left(\frac{x}{y}\right) = \frac{(-x)}{y} = \frac{x}{y}$

52. The table below shows Felix's bowling scores during the tournament. What is his average score?

Game	1	2	3	4	5
Score	290	300	225	235	270

F   255

G   264

H   265

J   273.75

53. Which of the following is the same as the sum of $-3\frac{1}{3} + 4\frac{8}{9}$?

A $-3 + \frac{1}{3} + 4 + \frac{8}{9}$

B $-3 - \frac{1}{3} - 4 + \frac{8}{9}$

C $3 + \frac{1}{3} - 4 - \frac{8}{9}$

D $-3 + -\frac{1}{3} + 4 + \frac{8}{9}$

54. Is $\frac{5}{0}$ a rational number? Choose the best answer.

F   No, 5 is not an integer.

G   No, the divisor is 0.

H   Yes, it is the quotient of two integers.

J   Yes, both 5 and 0 are integers.

55. Which of the following is an example of a number and its additive inverse?

A   A pitcher pitched a ball 18.39 m. The batter hit the ball 18.39 m toward first base.

B   A bird flew 10 miles from north to south and then 10 miles from west to east.

C   A contestant on a game show loses 30 points on the first question and wins 40 points on the second question.

D   A football team gains 35 yards on the first play and loses 35 yards on the second play.

56. Which of the following equations is true?

F $(5 + 7.3) + -2.7 = 5 + (7.3 - 2.7)$

G $(5 + 7.3) + -2.7 > 5 + (7.3 - 2.7)$

H $(5 + 7.3) - 2.7 \neq 5 + (7.3 - 2.7)$

J $(5 + 7.3) - 2.7 > 5 + (7.3 - 2.7)$

57. Which of the following statements is true?

A $\frac{2}{3}(-\frac{7}{11} + \frac{3}{4}) > -\frac{44}{33} + \frac{1}{2}$

B $\frac{2}{3}(-\frac{7}{11} + \frac{3}{4}) = -\frac{14}{33} + \frac{1}{2}$

C $\frac{2}{3}(-\frac{7}{11} + \frac{3}{4}) = \frac{14}{33} - \frac{1}{2}$

D $\frac{2}{3}(-\frac{7}{11} + \frac{3}{4}) = -\frac{14}{3} + \frac{1}{2}$

58. The temperature in Des Moines is $-10°F$. The temperature in Kansas City is 7 degrees colder. What is the temperature in Kansas City?

F $-17°F$

G $-3°F$

H $3°F$

J $17°F$

59. Which table does NOT show equivalent numbers?

A

$-\frac{1}{2}$	$\frac{-1}{2}$	$\frac{1}{-2}$

B

$\frac{1}{-4}$	$\frac{-1}{4}$	$-\frac{1}{4}$

C

$-\frac{1}{3}$	$\frac{1}{-3}$	$\frac{1}{3}$

D

$\frac{-1}{5}$	$-\frac{1}{5}$	$\frac{1}{-5}$

60. Ruth deposits $150.00 into her checking account. She then writes three checks, one for $65.75, one for $75.00, and one for $32.50. What is the net change in her checking account?

F $-\$23.25$

G $\$25.25$

H $-\$41.75$

J $\$108.25$

61. Find a, b, c, and d in the table below.

x	y	xy
+	−	a
−	b	−
c	+	+
−	d	+

A

a	b	c	d
−	+	+	−

B

a	b	c	d
+	−	+	+

C

a	b	c	d
−	+	−	−

D

a	b	c	d
+	−	+	−

62. Which of the following shows the opposites of 0, $-\frac{1}{3}$, 2.36, and $4\frac{2}{7}$?

F 0, $\frac{1}{3}$, -2.36, $4\frac{2}{7}$

G 0, $\frac{1}{3}$, -2.36, $-4\frac{2}{7}$

H 1, $-\frac{1}{3}$, -2.36, $-4\frac{2}{7}$

J -1, $-\frac{1}{3}$, 2.36, $-4\frac{2}{7}$

63. Is the number $3\frac{2}{3}$ a rational number? Why? Choose the best answer.

A Yes, the decimal form is 3.666…, and rational numbers can have repeating decimals.

B No, the decimal form is 3.666…, and rational numbers cannot have repeating decimals.

C Yes, the fraction can be expressed as 3.667.

D No, the number is greater than 1.

64. The volunteers at the hospital have 78 boxes to unpack. They figure they have unpacked $\frac{2}{3}$ of the boxes. How many are left to unpack?

F 26

G 39

H 52

J Not Here

65. What are the signs for a, b, and c in the table below?

x	y	$x + y, y > x$	$x + y, x > y$
+	−	a	+
−	+	+	b
−	−	c	−

A

a	b	c
−	−	−

B

a	b	c
+	−	−

C

a	b	c
+	+	−

D

a	b	c
−	+	+

66. Pun raises $64.50 for the school fund, Karl raises $50.60, and Michael raises $75.40. How much do they raise in all?

F $115.10

G $126.00

H $139.90

J $190.50

67. What are the additive inverse and opposite of −23?

   A The additive inverse is 23, and the opposite is 32.

   B The additive inverse is −23, and the opposite is 23.

   C The additive inverse is 23, and the opposite is 23.

   D The additive inverse is 32, and the opposite is −23.

68. The top of Mount Elbrus in Russia is 18,510 feet above sea level. Lake Eyre in Australia is −49 feet below sea level. How far is it from the top of Mt. Elbrus to the bottom of Lake Eyre?

   F −18,559 feet

   G −18,461 feet

   H 18,461 feet

   J 18,559 feet

69. The hottest temperature in Asia was 55°C in Mitraba, Kuwait. The coldest measured temperature in Asia was −67.8°C in Siberia, Russia. What is the net change in temperature from the hottest to the coldest?

   A −122.8°C

   B −12.8°C

   C 12.8°C

   D 122.8°C

70. Which of the following rules will give the correct sign to the quotient of $4\frac{7}{12} \div -5\frac{1}{2}$?

   F The quotient of a positive and a negative number is positive.

   G The quotient of a positive and a negative number is negative.

   H The quotient of two positive numbers is positive.

   J The quotient of two negative numbers is negative.

71. Bob's checking account balance is $153.70. His account has overdraft protection if he withdraws more than his balance, but the bank charges $12.00 for covering each overdraft transaction. Bob makes the following four withdrawals in this order: $50.47, $75.30, $30.00, $50.40. What is his balance?

   A −$76.47

   B −$66.54

   C −$52.48

   D −$40.47

72. Which of the following is the correct example for the expression: $150 + -150 = 0$?

   F Walter opens a checking account with a deposit of $150.00. During the first week he makes ATM withdrawals totaling $150.00. What is his balance?

   G A bus travels 150 miles on Monday and 150 miles on Tuesday. What is the total number of miles traveled by the bus?

   H A movie theater has 150 people. Almost all of them leave after the first movie. How many remain in the theater?

   J Rita raises $150.00 for the 5K race. Jan also raises $150.00. What is their total?

73. The alumni group has its annual charity drive and raises $50,213.00 in April. In May, it totals up all the expenses. The total is $57,500.00. What is the net gain or loss for the charity drive?

   A −$107,713.00

   B −$7,287.00

   C $7,287.00

   D $107,713.00

74. The drop in temperature from 12:00 P.M. to 6:00 P.M. is 17°F. What is the average hourly drop for this time period?

   F −2.4284°F

   G −2.8333…°F

   H 3.4°F

   J Not Here

75. What is the value of this expression as a decimal?

$$\frac{1\frac{1}{2} + 2\frac{3}{4} - 6\frac{1}{8}}{3\frac{1}{5}}$$

   A −7.375

   B −0.5859

   C 0.5859

   D 10.375

Name _____ Date _____

Expressions and Equations

Modeled Instruction

DIRECTIONS: Read each question and choose the best answer. Use the answer sheet provided at the end of the workbook to record your answers. If the correct answer is not available, mark the letter for "Not Here."

1. Mrs. Mata's class has 35 students. Her principal tells her that the maximum allowed in the class is 30 students, so 5 students must be transferred out of her class. Which equation yields the percent decrease?

    A $35 - x = 30$

    B $35 - 35x = 30$

    C $30 - 35x = 35$

    D $30 = 35x$

     Hint

    The percent decrease is x. The student decrease is 5. The class starts with 35 students.

2. Paula is packing her photo albums into 5 boxes. There are at least 10 albums in each box. Which is the correct inequality to find out how many albums she has?

    F $\frac{a}{5} \le 10$

    G $\frac{a}{5} < 10$

    H $\frac{a}{5} \ge 10$

    J $\frac{a}{5} > 10$

     Hint

    When you see the phrase "at least," think about the inequality sign you should use.

3. Many retail stores mark up their merchandise by 50% of their cost. If the cost per item is $3.25, what is the selling price?

    A $1.63

    B $2.44

    C $3.90

    D $4.88

     Hint

    Find 50% of the cost and add it to the cost to find the selling price.

4. Solve for x.

    $6(4x - 5) = 36$

    F $x = 0.25$

    G $x = 1.708$

    H $x = 2.75$

    J $x = 16.5$

     Hint

    Use the Distributive Property. Then solve for x.

5. The perimeter of the garage is 64 feet. The length is 20 feet. What is the width of the garage?

   A 1.6 ft

   B 12 ft

   C 24 ft

   D 44 ft

   Hint

   The formula for the perimeter of a rectangle is $p = 2(l + w)$. Substitute the known values in the formula and solve for the unknown.

6. Tom's Bike Shop is selling bicycles at a 33% discount if people pay with cash. Which equation can be used to compute this special price?

   F $0.67b$

   G $0.33b$

   H $33b$

   J $67b$

   Hint

   If the discount is 33%, the sale price is 100% − 33%.

7. Which of the following is the factored form of $5x + 30$?

   A $5(x + 30)$

   B $5(x + 25)$

   C $5(x - 6)$

   D $5(x + 6)$

   Hint

   Find the largest number that is a factor of both 5 and 30.

8. Tuition today is $4,300.00 per semester. Next year there will be a 2.5% increase. How much will tuition be next year?

   F $4,310.75

   G $4,407.50

   H $5,375.00

   J $15,050.00

   Hint

   Multiply the cost by the percent converted to a decimal. Add this to the original cost.

9. Mary buys $4\frac{2}{3}$ yards of material for less than $75.00. How much is the material per yard?

   A greater than $16.07 per yard

   B $16.07 per yard

   C less than $16.07 per yard

   D less than or equal to $16.07 per yard

Hint

Write an inequality based on what she buys and pays.

10. Combine $(4x - 1\frac{1}{2}) - (20x + 3\frac{7}{8})$.

   F $-(16x + 5\frac{3}{8})$

   G $16x + 5\frac{3}{8}$

   H $16x - 5\frac{3}{8}$

   J $-(16x - 5\frac{3}{8})$

Hint

Use the Distributive Property to eliminate the parentheses and then combine like terms.

11. Hazel buys silk flower arrangements for resale. She marks up her sales price by 25%. Which two expressions represent the selling price (p) of the arrangements?

   A $p + 0.25p$ and $1 + 25p$

   B $2.5p$ and $1.25p$

   C $2.5p$ and $1.025p$

   D $p + 0.25p$ and $1.25p$

Hint

The selling price is her cost plus 25% of her cost.

12. Solve the equation $3(-4\frac{3}{5} - 5x) = 360$.

   F $x = -24.92$

   G $x = -23.08$

   H $x = 23.08$

   J $x = 24.92$

Hint

Use the Distributive Property and then add and divide both sides of the equation by the same numbers.

13. Mylene is hanging a mirror and wants to center it on the wall. The mirror is 36 inches long, and the wall is 72 inches long from corner to corner. What is the distance from the corner to the edge of the mirror?

  A   18 in.

  B   27 in.

  C   36 in.

  D   54 in.

 Hint

Subtract the length of the mirror from the wall measurement and divide by 2.

14. Bella sells half the CDs in her library. After that, she buys 4 more CDs. She now has 80 CDs. How many did she have to start with?

  F   138

  G   152

  H   182

  J   Not Here

 Hint

Write and solve an equation representing what you know about her CDs. To solve, perform the same operations on both sides of the equation.

15. Which of the following is the graph of $11x \geq -22$?

  A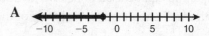

  B

  C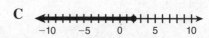

  D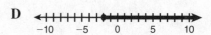

 Hint

Solve for x. Think about the difference between graphing an equation and an inequality.

16. Hasan sells movie tickets. Adult tickets cost $12.50, and student/senior tickets cost $11.00. He keeps 10% of his sales. Which expression represents how much he keeps?

  F $10(12.50a + 11.00s)$

  G $0.10(23.50as)$

  H $0.10(12.50a + 11.00s)$

  J $12.50a + 11.00s$

 Hint

Take 10% of the total number of tickets sold.

17. A table is being centered on a wall. The wall is 8.1 feet long, and the table is 5.4 feet long. Which equation can be used to determine how much of the wall should be on each side of the table?

A $8.1 - 5.4x = 2$

B $5.4x - 2 = 8.1$

C $2x - 5.4 = 8.1$

D $8.1 - 2x = 5.4$

 Hint

Subtract the table measure from the wall measure and divide by 2.

18. The price for mailing a package is $1.28 for the first ounce and $0.84 for each additional ounce. Sandra pays $13.88 to mail her package. How much does it weigh?

F 16 ounces

G 20 ounces

H 24 ounces

J 28 ounces

 Hint

Subtract the cost of one ounce from the total and then divide the remaining number by the price per ounce.

19. Sara sells baseball caps for *s* dollars. For her summer sale, she reduces the price by 25%. Which expression represents the sale price of the caps?

A $1.25s$

B $0.75s$

C $1.75s$

D $0.25s$

 Hint

Since the discount is 25%, find how much she is making on each cap.

20. Tomás is buying DVDs. Each DVD costs $14.95, and there is an 8.25% sales tax. How many DVDs does he buy with $75.00, and how much does he have left?

F He buys 5 and has $10.91 left.

G He buys 5 and has nothing left.

H He buys 4 and has $20.66 left.

J He buys 4 and has $10.26 left.

 Hint

Divide the total he spends by the cost of each DVD. Then estimate the number he buys and find the cost with tax. Subtract from what he can spend. Re-estimate as necessary.

21. Shauna makes $11.50 per hour. Her boss tells her she is getting a 4.5% raise. How much will Shauna make working a 40-hour week?

A $439.30

B $454.82

C $480.70

D $667.00

Hint

Find the new hourly rate and multiply by the number of hours in the week.

22. If the volume of a sphere is 36π, what is the length of the radius?

F $\sqrt{2}$

G   3

H 3π

J   27

Hint

The formula for the volume of a sphere is $V = \frac{4}{3}\pi r^3$. Replace the unknowns in the formula with the information given in the problem and then solve for r.

23. A brother and a sister set up a food booth and a game booth at the local street fair. The fee for the food booth is $50.00 plus $10.00 per day. The fee for the game booth is $25.00 plus $15.00 per day. What is the difference in the total cost between the two booths for 5 days?

A $0

B $25.00

C $40.00

D $60.00

Hint

Compute each weekly cost and compare the results.

24. Elroy has $500.00 to spend on sports equipment. Softballs cost $10.00, bats cost $100.00, and footballs cost $20.00. Elroy needs 7 softballs and 5 footballs. How many bats can he buy, and how much will he have left?

F   He can buy 3.3 bats and will have $0 left.

G   He can buy 3 bats and have $30.00 left.

H   He can buy 3 bats and have $70.00 left.

J   He can buy 3 bats and have $100.00 left.

Hint

Write and solve an inequality using the information you know about what must be purchased. Remember, you cannot buy part of a bat.

25. The Performing Arts Center has seats in the areas listed in the table.

Type of Seat	Number of Seats
Orchestra	1,000
Mezzanine	800
Balcony	400

Suppose all the Orchestra seats are sold. Which inequality will determine how many seats are vacant and can be sold in the Performing Arts Center?

A $1,000 + s \leq 1,800$

B $1,000 + s \leq 2,200$

C $1,000 + s \geq 2,200$

D $1,000 + s \geq 1,200$

Hint

The number sold plus what can be sold equals the total.

Expressions and Equations

Independent Practice

DIRECTIONS: Read each question and choose the best answer. Use the answer sheet provided at the end of the workbook to record your answers. If the correct answer is not available, mark the letter for "Not Here."

26. Marta's business marks up prices on the chairs it sells. She buys s chairs from her supplier. She marks up the chairs by 45%. Which expression gives her selling price for one chair?

    F $s - 1.45$

    G $1.45s$

    H $s + 1.45$

    J $s \div 1.45$

27. Zena and Audrey are on the same bowling team. The sum of their averages is 299. If Zena's average is 13 pins greater than Audrey's average, what is Zena's average?

    A 104

    B 119

    C 156

    D 169

28. At the beginning of the year, one share of stock was worth $62.00. By the end of the year, its value had increased 27%. What is the value of the stock at the end of the year?

    F $16.74

    G $62.78

    H $78.74

    J $107.26

29. Combine $y - 8 + 3(y + 4)$.

    A $4y - 4$

    B $4y + 4$

    C $4y + 20$

    D $2y + 20$

30. The width of a rectangle is 3 feet shorter than its length. Which of the following is the perimeter of the rectangle?

    F $2l - 3$

    G $4l + 6$

    H $4l - 3$

    J $4l - 6$

31. Jane sells hats. For a sale, she marks them down 20%. If her original selling price is $59.95 per hat, what is her sale price?

    A $11.99

    B $12.00

    C $47.96

    D $48.00

32. Solve the equation.

$$4(-6x - 8) = 208$$

F $x = -10$

G $x = -7.333\ldots$

H $x = 7.333\ldots$

J $x = 10$

33. Which of the following correctly completes the table?

Inequality	Multiply Each Side by	Correct New Inequality
$-10 \leq -1$	4	a
$1 \leq 12$	-3	b

A

a	b
$-10 \leq -4$	$-3 \leq -12$

B

a	b
$-40 \leq -4$	$-3 \geq -36$

C

a	b
$-10 \geq -4$	$-3 \geq -12$

D

a	b
$-40 \geq -4$	$-3 < -36$

34. Gary and Mike are on the same swim team. Gary swims 3 times as many laps as Mike, plus 5 more laps. Gary swims 35 laps. How many laps does Mike swim?

F 7

G 10

H 13

J 17

35. Perla reads 3 less than 5 times the number of books Nancy reads. Which equation represents the number of books Perla reads?

A $5n + 3 = p$

B $3n - 5 = p$

C $5n - 3 = p$

D $3n + 5 = p$

36. A town has a population of 16,355. The chamber of commerce wants to know what percent increase would be necessary for the town's population to be at least 20,000.

F 18.22%

G 22.28%

H 77.72%

J 81.78%

37. Each week Bernardo gets an allowance of $5.00; plus he gets $3.00 for each chore he does around the house. Bernardo's sister gets $6.00 as an allowance and $2.00 for each chore. If each one does 15 chores during the week, how much money do they get altogether?

   A $14.00

   B $36.00

   C $50.00

   D $86.00

38. A picture is being centered on a wall. The wall is 7.8 feet from corner to corner. The picture is 3.4 feet long. Which equation can be used to determine how far from the corner the edge of the picture will be?

   F $3.4x - 1 = 7.8$

   G $7.8 - 2x = 3.4$

   H $2x - 3.4 = 7.8$

   J $7.8 - 3.4x = 2$

39. Mrs. Chung buys 5 cups of coffee at a kiosk in the mall. The bill is less than $20.00. What is the cost of each cup?

   A less than $4.00

   B greater than $4.00

   C equal to $4.00

   D less than or equal to $4.00

40. The perimeter of the infield of a baseball field is 360 feet. If the length is 90 feet, what is the width of the infield?

   F 90 ft

   G 180 ft

   H 270 ft

   J Not Here

41. A company has 3,025 workers. The president of the company tells the city council that the number will be at least 4,000 in five years. What percent increase is this?

   A 24.37%

   B 32.23%

   C 67.77%

   D 75.26%

42. A group of 10 people goes out to eat. They decide to split the bill so each person pays $\frac{1}{10}$ of the total price. Appetizers are $7.00, and main dishes are $12.00. Everyone orders 1 of each. When the check comes, it includes a 15% tip. How much does each person pay?

   F $13.80

   G $19.00

   H $19.28

   J $21.85

43. Rachel sells $\frac{1}{3}$ of her stamp collection. She then buys 10 more stamps. She now has 1,253 stamps in her collection. How many stamps did she have to start with?

A 3,789

B 3,730

C 1,263

D Not Here

44. Simplify the expression.

$2t + 5 - 8t - 2$

F $10t + 7$

G $10t - 7$

H $-6t + 3$

J $-6t - 3$

45. Which of the following is the graph of $4x \geq -28$?

A

B

C

D

46. Let p equal the price of a CD. There is a sales tax of 4.53%. Which expression represents the total for 5 CDs?

F $p + 1.0453p$

G $p \times 1.0453p$

H $5(p + 0.0453p)$

J $5p \times 1.0453p$

47. Mr. Barrera makes \$40,523.00 a year. Everyone in the company is getting an 8.4% increase. How much is Mr. Barrera going to make, to the nearest dollar?

A \$3,403.00

B \$37,119.00

C \$43,927.00

D \$47,329.00

48. As a server, Jake is paid \$100.00 a week plus \$15.00 for each table of more than 4 people he serves. This week he wants to make at least \$150.00. Which inequality should he use to determine how many tables of more than 4 people he needs to serve?

F $15x + 150 \geq 100$

G $15x + 100 \leq 150$

H $15x + 100 \geq 150$

J $15x + 150 \leq 150$

49. Jamil sells books. Hardcover books are $14.95 each. Paperback books are $8.95 each. He keeps 25% of his sales. If he sells 4 hardcover books and 5 paperback books, how much does he earn?

    A $11.18 **B** $14.95 **C** $26.14 **D** $78.41

50. Solve the inequality.

$$-\frac{x}{7} + 21 < -14$$

    F $x > -245$

    G $x < -245$

    H $x < 245$

    J $x > 245$

51. Your parents say that you can spend at most $200.00 on summer activities. From the list in the table, you have chosen the amusement park and the pool passes. You also want to go camping. How many camping trips can you go on, and will you have enough money to choose another activity from the table?

Summer Activity	Cost
Amusement Park Pass	$45
Season Pool Pass	$50
Zoo Yearly Pass	$45
Basketball Camp	$145
Camping Trip	$75

    A You can go on 1.57 camping trips, and you will not be able to do anything else.

    B You can go on 1 camping trip, and you will be able to do something else.

    C You can go on 1.57 camping trips, and you will be able to do something else.

    D You can go on 1 camping trip, and you will not be able to do anything else.

52. The price for shipping a package is $3.00 for the first 3 kilograms and $1.50 for each additional kilogram. Rafael pays $27.36 to ship his package. How much does it weigh?

    F 6.08 kilograms

    G 19.24 kilograms

    H 22.86 kilograms

    J 31.86 kilograms

53. Jaida sells fertilizer for outdoor plants. Her 5-pound bag sells for $15.00, her 10-pound bag for $25.00, and her 50-pound bag for $100.00. How much does she make if she sells an equal number of each size?

    A $140n$

    B $125n$

    C $400n$

    D $60n$

54. Bert earns $12.35 per hour. His boss promises him a raise of 2.2%. How much more will he earn in a 40-hour week?

    F $0.27

    G $10.87

    H $494.00

    J $504.87

55. Gloria sells skateboards. For her winter sale, she marks them down by 40%. If her regular price for one skateboard is $89.00 each, how much does she make if she sells 25 at the sale price?

   A $133.50

   B $890.00

   C $1,335.00

   D   Not Here

56. If the volume of a prism is 500 cubic feet and the height is 5 feet, how long is each side of the square base?

   F   5 feet

   G   10 feet

   H   15 feet

   J   100 feet

57. Simplify the expression $4(x - 3) + 5(x - 3)$.

   A $9x + 27$

   B $9x - 27$

   C $-9 + 27x$

   D $-9 - 27x$

58. Lamar is putting a new baseboard around his bedroom. The perimeter of the room is $75\frac{1}{2}$ feet. He measures the width and finds that it is $15\frac{3}{4}$ feet. What is the length?

   F   19.5 feet

   G   22 feet

   H   22.37 feet

   J   44 feet

59. Tony has $68.00 to spend on two CDs and a CD player. The two CDs cost the same amount. The CD player is $20.00. Which inequality indicates how much he can spend on each CD?

   A $x \geq 24$

   B $x \leq 40$

   C $x \leq 24$

   D $x \geq 40$

60. Tai buys and sells used car parts. He marks up his sale price by 55%. Which of the following shows two expressions that represent the selling price?

   F $p + 0.55p$ and $1 + 55p$

   G $p + 55p$ and $1.55p$

   H $p + 0.55p$ and $1.55p$

   J $p + 5.5p$ and $1.055p$

61. Romelia buys and sells laptop computers. She keeps 40% of the selling price. If she sells a laptop for $750.00, how much does she keep?

A $214.29

B $300.00

C $450.00

D $535.71

62. Eduardo is buying picture frames for his photography business. Each picture frame costs $8.95. Because he resells them, there is no tax. How many frames can he buy with $100.00, and how much money will he have left? Remember, he can only buy whole frames.

F He can buy 11.17 and will have no money left.

G He can buy 10 and will have $10.50 left.

H He can buy 11 and will have $2.55 left.

J Not Here

63. One school has 1,100 students. When this school combines with another school that is closing, there will be a total of 1,900 students. Which equation can be used to find the percent increase?

A $1,100 + x = 1,900$

B $1,100 + 1,100x = 1,900$

C $1,900 - 1,100x = x$

D $1,100x = 1,900$

64. The ballpark has seats in the areas listed in the table.

Type	Number
Box	10
Reserved	20,000
General Admission	22,000
Bleachers	7,990

Suppose all the box and reserved seats have been sold. Which inequality will determine how many seats remain to be sold?

F $29,990 + s \le 50,000$

G $50,000 + s \le 29,990$

H $29,990 + s \ge 50,000$

J $20,010 + s \le 50,000$

65. Esther buys and sells video games. She pays between $2.50 and $3.00 each and sells them for 60% more. What is her selling price?

A between $3.50 and $4.20

B between $4.00 and $5.00

C between $3.75 and $4.80

D between $4.00 and $4.80

66. The local moving company is giving an estimate on moving an office. The price for the first 100 pounds is $300.00. Each additional 100 pounds is $150.00. The moving company charges $5,376.00 for the move. How many pounds are being moved?

F 33.84 pounds

G 133.84 pounds

H 3,484 pounds

J 3,384 pounds

67. Tanisha has a square dining room that is 12 feet on each side. She wants to center a rug in the room. The rug is 8 feet by 8 feet. How far from each wall should she place the rug?

A   2 feet

B   2.5 feet

C   3 feet

D   4 feet

68. Eugene buys and sells MP3 players. He purchases 50 MP3 players for $1,000.00. He marks them up 30% before selling them. What is his selling price for each MP3 player?

F $6.00

G $13.00

H $26.00

J $300.00

69. Solve the inequality.

$0.8 \geq -3.5x - 9.2$

A $-2.857 \leq x$

B $2,857 \geq x$

C $-2.857 \geq x$

D $2.857 \leq x$

70. A company's monthly payroll is $60,562.00. The company will have an across-the-board 3.5% increase in salaries next year. What will the monthly payroll be next year?

F $2,119.67

G $62,681.67

H $64,801.34

J   Not Here

71. The Galindo Company had 750 employees in 2011. For 2012, there will likely be a 12% increase. How many employees is the company expecting to have in 2012?

A   800

B   840

C   910

D   Not Here

72. In March, gold sells for $1,513.00 per ounce. Six months later, gold sells for $1,750.00 per ounce. What is the percent increase?

F   13.54%

G   15.66%

H   86.45%

J   115.66%

73. An artist sets up a booth at an art fair. The fee is $200.00 plus a 15% commission on everything she sells. If her sales are $1,250.00, how much does she pay for the booth?

A $187.50

B $200.00

C $387.50

D $1,280.00

74. A mover notes the weight of a bed and 2 side tables and records it as $b + 2c \geq 200$ on his invoice. What is he communicating?

F   The bed and night tables each weigh more than 200 pounds.

G   The bed and night tables weigh at most 200 pounds.

H   The bed and night tables weigh approximately 200 pounds or less.

J   The bed and night tables weigh at least 200 pounds.

75. Jacklyn sells tablecloths. For her holiday sale, she marks everything down by 15%. Which two expressions represent the price of the tablecloths?

A $p + 0.15p$ and $0.85p$

B $p + 0.85p$ and $0.15p$

C $p - 0.85p$ and $0.15p$

D $p - 0.15p$ and $0.85p$

Geometry

Modeled Instruction

DIRECTIONS: Read each question and choose the best answer. Use the answer sheet provided at the end of the workbook to record your answers. If the correct answer is not available, mark the letter for "Not Here."

1. Find the surface area of a rectangular solid with these dimensions: length 11 in., width 3 in., and height 6 in.

   A 135 square inches   **B** 234 square inches   **C** 332 square inches   **D** 798 square inches

 Hint

   Find the sum of the areas of the six sides.

---

2. Look at the figure below.

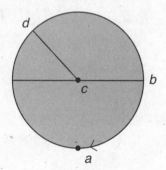

   Which of the following is the correct way to label the circle?

   F

a	*b*	*c*	*d*
diameter	radius	center	circumference

   H

a	*b*	*c*	*d*
circumference	diameter	center	radius

   G

a	*b*	*c*	*d*
diameter	center	circumference	radius

   J

a	*b*	*c*	*d*
center	circumference	radius	diameter

 Hint

   Think about the definition of the terms related to a circle.

Name _____ **Date** _____

3. Look at this figure.

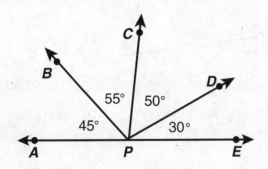

Which two angles are NOT supplementary?

A ∠APC and ∠CPE

B ∠DPE and ∠DPA

C ∠DPC and ∠CPB

D ∠EPB and ∠BPA

Hint

Supplementary angles have measures that add up to 180°.

4. Rosa is painting a dresser that measures 8 feet long by 2.5 feet wide by 3 feet high. How many square feet will she paint if she paints all the surfaces except the bottom?

F 50 square feet

G 83 square feet

H 98 square feet

J 103 square feet

Hint

Find the sum of the areas of the 5 surfaces she is painting.

5. The table below shows different ways a cone and a plane can intersect.

Intersection	Figure Formed
Plane parallel to the base	a
Plane through the vertex and crossing the base	b
Plane not parallel to the base	c

Which of the following is true of a, b, and c?

A

a	b	c
circle	rectangle	oval

B

a	b	c
square	triangle	oval

C

a	b	c
circle	triangle	oval

D

a	b	c
oval	triangle	circle

Hint

Draw the intersection described in the table and analyze your results.

6. The scale on a blueprint is 2 cm:3 m. If an actual room measures 4 meters by 3 meters, what are the dimensions of the room on the blueprint?

F 6 cm by 4.5 cm

G 2.67 cm by 2 cm

H 6 cm by 2 cm

J 2.67 cm by 6 cm

Hint

Set up proportions with the known information and solve for the information you need to know.

7. A plane intersects a triangular prism, forming a triangle and a trapezoid, as shown in the figure below.

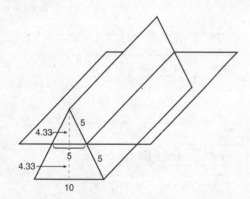

What is the difference between the area of the trapezoid and the area of the triangle?

A 0 square feet

C 21.65 square feet

B 8.66 square feet

D 43.29 square feet

Hint

Find the areas of the two figures and then subtract to find the difference.

8. Look at this diagram.

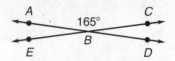

Which of the following does NOT name a pair of vertical angles?

F ∠ABC and ∠EBD

G ∠ABE and ∠CBD

H ∠CBA and ∠DBE

J ∠ABC and ∠ABE

Hint

Vertical angles are opposite angles when two lines intersect.

9. Look at the figure below.

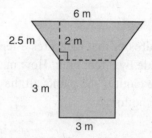

If carpet costs $24.50 per square meter, how much will it cost to carpet the area shown?

A $490.00   **C** $533.40

B $441.00   **D** $661.50

Hint

Divide the figure into rectangles, squares, and triangles. Find the sum of the areas of each segment. Multiply by the cost of the carpet.

10. Look at the figure below.

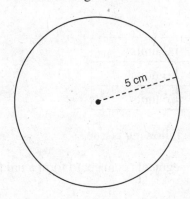

What is the circumference of the circle?

F 2.5π   **G** 5π   **H** 10π   **J** 25π

Hint

The formula for the circumference of a circle is π*d* or 2π*r*.

---

11. Use the map of Florida to estimate the distance between Tallahassee and Miami.

A 458 km   **B** 600 km   **C** 660 km   **D** 720 km

Hint

Set up a proportion with the known information and solve for the information you need to know.

12. If a trapezoid and a triangle are formed by the intersection of a triangular prism and a plane, which of the following describes how the two intersect?

   F   parallel to one of the rectangular sides

   G   through one of the vertices

   H   perpendicular to one of the rectangular sides

   J   parallel to the triangular sides

Hint

Fold a sheet of paper into a triangular prism. Intersect it with another sheet of paper and evaluate the result.

13. Look at the table.

Actual Alligator Length	Scale Drawing
15 feet	30 inches

What is the scale?

   A   1:24   **C**   1:12

   B   1:6   **D**   1:2

Hint

Set up a ratio with the known information and reduce to lowest terms.

14. The table gives the measurements of three line segments.

Segment 1	2 units
Segment 2	3 units
Segment 3	6 units

Which of the following is true?

   F   The line segments connect to form a unique triangle.

   G   The line segments connect to form more than one triangle.

   H   The line segments do not connect, and a triangle cannot be formed.

   J   The line segments connect to form exactly two triangles.

Hint

Two shorter sides of a triangle must be longer than the third side.

15. Look at the figure below.

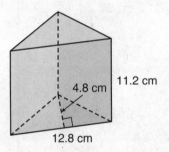

Find the volume.

   A   143.36 cm³   **C**   286.72 cm³

   B   344.064 cm³   **D**   573.44 cm³

Hint

$V = \frac{1}{2} Bh$, where B is the area of the base and h is the height.

16. Which figure CANNOT have a rectangular cross section?

F prism

G cone

H cube

J cylinder

Hint

Draw each figure and imagine the intersection with the plane.

17. The circumference of a circular garden is 30 meters. A gardener is using a machine to dig a straight line along the diameter of the garden at a rate of 5 meters per hour. About how long will it take to dig across the garden? Use $\pi = 3.14$.

A about 1 hour

B about 2 hours

C about 3.8 hours

D about 4.5 hours

Hint

Find the length of the diameter and then divide by the digging speed.

18. Toni is going to varnish the top of a circular table. If the radius of the table is 27 inches and a can of varnish covers 25 square feet, how many cans will Toni need? Use $\pi = 3.14$.

F 0.5 can

G 1 can

H 1.5 cans

J 2 cans

Hint

Use the formula to find the area of the table. Remember, paint only comes in whole cans.

19. Look at the figure below.

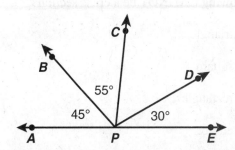

Which equation will give the measure of $\angle CPD$?

A $\angle CPD + 55° + 45° + 30° = 180°$

B $\angle CPD + 55° = 90°$

C $\angle CPD + 55° + 45° + 90° = 180°$

D Not Here

Hint

Angles *APB, BPC, CPD,* and *DPE* are supplementary.

20. On a map, two cities measure 5.2 inches apart. The scale of the map is 2 in.:16 miles. What is the actual distance between the two cities?

F 40.8 miles

G 41.6 miles

H 63.4 miles

J 83.2 miles

Hint

Set up a proportion with the known information and solve for the information you need to know.

21. If a plane intersects a cube, which of the following CANNOT be a cross section?

A triangle

B square

C rectangle

D circle

Hint

Think about the shapes that can be drawn with straight lines.

22. You are given angle measures of 30°, 60°, and 90°. Which of the following is true?

F You can draw a unique triangle.

G You can draw more than one triangle.

H You cannot have a triangle with these angle measures.

J You can draw exactly two triangles.

Hint

Try drawing different triangles with these angle measures.

23. The highway intersects Avenue A and 77th Street, as shown in the figure below. If ∠B is greater than 35°, the city will allow parks to be built on both sides of the highway.

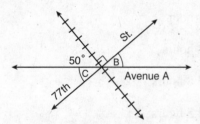

Can parks be built in ∠B and ∠C? Why?

A Yes, the angles measure greater than 35° each.

B No, the angles measure less than 35° each.

C Yes, at ∠B but not at angle C because ∠A > 35° but ∠B < 35°.

D Not Here

Hint

Use the relationships between vertical angles and supplementary angles.

24. Look at the figure.

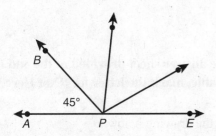

Which of the following is NOT true?

F   ∠*APB* and ∠*BPE* are supplementary angles.

G   ∠*BPE* measures 135°.

H   ∠*APB* is an acute angle.

J   ∠*APB* and ∠*BPE* are complementary angles.

Hint

Think about the angles that are formed when two lines intersect.

25. Look at the figure below.

Which of the following is true?

A   ∠*ABC* measures 55°.

B   The protractor is not placed correctly to measure ∠*ABC*.

C   ∠*ABC* measures 125°.

D   The protractor measures the length of the line segments *AB* and *BC*.

Hint

Think about how to read a protractor. The smaller the angle, the smaller is its measure.

Name _____ Date _____

Geometry

Independent Practice

DIRECTIONS: Read each question and choose the best answer. Use the answer sheet provided at the end of the workbook to record your answers. If the correct answer is not available, mark the letter for "Not Here."

26. The table shows the length of three line segments.

Segment 1	4 inches
Segment 2	5 inches
Segment 3	6 inches

Which of the following is a true statement?

F The line segments connect to form a unique triangle.

G The line segments connect to form more than one triangle.

H The line segments do not connect, and a triangle cannot be formed.

J The line segments connect to form exactly two triangles.

27. Which of the following is the volume of a rectangular prism 6 cm long, 3 cm wide, and 6 cm high?

A 102 cm³

B 108 cm³

C 112 cm³

D 118 cm³

28. Look at the drawing below.

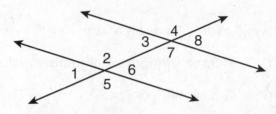

Which of the following identifies pairs of vertical angles?

F angles 1 and 5, 2 and 6, 3 and 8, 4 and 7

G angles 1 and 6, 2 and 5, 4 and 7, 3 and 7

H angles 1 and 2, 2 and 5, 1 and 6, 3 and 8, 3 and 7

J angles 1 and 6, 2 and 5, 3 and 8, 4 and 7

29. The table below shows different ways a cylinder and a plane can intersect.

Intersection	Figure Formed
The plane intersects the circular bases.	*a*
The plane is parallel to the circular bases.	*b*
The plane is not parallel to the circular bases.	*c*

Which of the following is true of *a*, *b*, and *c*?

A

a	*b*	*c*
circle	oval	rectangle

C

a	*b*	*c*
oval	circle	rectangle

B

a	*b*	*c*
rectangle	oval	circle

D

a	*b*	*c*
rectangle	circle	oval

30. Marisa measures the deck on the outside of the house and makes a scale drawing with a scale of 1 cm:6 m. The actual deck is 18 m long. How long is it in the drawing?

F 0.33 cm   **G** 3 cm   **H** 18 cm   **J** 108 cm

31. The area of a circle is 25π square inches. What is the circumference?

A 5π **B** 10π **C** 25π **D** 156.25

32. Three segments have measurements of 3 inches, 6 inches, and 12 inches. Which of the following is true?

F The line segments connect to form a unique triangle.

G The line segments connect to form more than one triangle.

H The line segments do not connect, and a triangle cannot be formed.

J The line segments connect to form exactly two triangles.

33. The radius of a cylindrical juice can is 1.5 inches, and the height is 5 inches. What is the volume? Use $\pi = 3.14$.

A 35.33 in.^{3}

B 47.10 in.^{3}

C 55.46 in.^{3}

D 110.92 in.^{3}

34. The known angles in a triangle measure 65° and 35°. Which equation will give the measurement of the third angle?

F $a = 90 - 65$

G $a = 180 - (65 + 35)$

H $a = 90 - 35$

J $a = 180 + (65 - 35)$

35. A manufacturer ships dolls in boxes that measure 2 in. × 3 in. × 4 in. If he packages 96 doll boxes in a shipping carton that measures 12 in. × 15 in. × 15 in., how much space is left for packing material?

A 396 in.^{3}

B 2,304 in.^{3}

C 2,676 in.^{3}

D 2,700 in.^{3}

36. Look at the figure below.

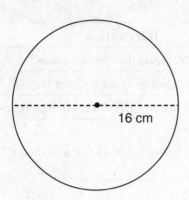

16 cm

Which of the following gives the correct circumference and area of the circle?

F $C = 8\pi, A = 16\pi$

G $C = 64\pi, A = 16\pi$

H $C = 8\pi, A = 64\pi$

J $C = 16\pi, A = 64\pi$

37. Look at the figure below.

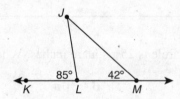

What is the measure of $\angle J$?

A 43°

B 95°

C 127°

D 137°

38. Which two figures can have a circle cross section?

F cone and prism

G cone and cylinder

H cube and cylinder

J cube and prism

39. If a triangular prism is intersected by a plane parallel to one of the rectangular sides, what two figures are formed?

A trapezoid and triangle

B circle and rectangle

C trapezoid and rectangle

D triangle and cube

40. If a plane intersects a square pyramid, which of the following CANNOT be a cross section?

F trapezoid

G triangle

H oval

J square

41. Jeremy is making a blueprint of a building. He is using a scale of 1 in.:3 ft. One wall of a room measures 33 feet. How long will he draw it in his blueprint?

A 0.27 in.

B 3 in.

C 3.66 in.

D 11 in.

42. The diameter of a circular garden is 25 feet. A gardener is using a machine to dig a trench all around the garden. The machine moves at 10 feet per hour. About how long will it take to dig around the garden? Use $\pi = 3.14$.

F 3.92 hours

G 7.85 hours

H 12.4 hours

J 15.62 hours

43. A geometric solid is intersected by a plane. Some of the possible cross sections are triangle, square, rectangle, trapezoid, and parallelogram. What is the geometric solid?

A cylinder

B cube

C cone

D triangular pyramid

44. Look at the figure below.

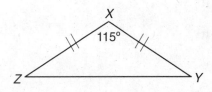

What is the measure of $\angle Y$?

F 25°

G 32.5°

H 65°

J 75°

45. On a map, the distance between Hershey, Pennsylvania, and Pittsburg, Pennsylvania, is 3.5 inches. The actual mileage is 175 miles. What is the scale being used?

A   1 in.:35 mi

B   1 in.:50 mi

C   1 in.:58.33 mi

D   1 in.:171.5 mi

46. Anne is painting a bedroom wall 9 ft high and 15 ft long. She won't paint the two windows shown by gray rectangles in the figure below. What is the area of what she is going to paint?

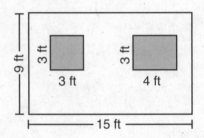

F   114 ft^2

G   117 ft^2

H   124 ft^2

J   135 ft^2

47. You are given three line segments that measure 3 cm, 6 cm, and 10 cm. Which statement is true?

A   The line segments connect to form a unique triangle.

B   The line segments do not connect, and a triangle cannot be formed.

C   The line segments connect to form more than one triangle.

D   The line segments connect to form exactly two triangles.

48. Roger is making a cover for a circular pool. If the diameter of the pool is 6 feet, what are the circumference and area of the pool cover, assuming it fits exactly on top of the pool? Use $\pi = 3.14$.

F $C = 28.26$ ft, $A = 18.84$ ft^2

G $C = 188.4$ ft, $A = 28.26$ ft^2

H $C = 18.84$ ft, $A = 282.6$ ft^2

J $C = 18.84$ ft, $A = 28.26$ ft^2

49. The table below shows the relationship between the length of a circle's diameter in inches and the length of its circumference in inches. Use $\pi = 3.14$.

Diameter (in.)	4	5	6	7
Circumference (in.)	12.56	15.7	18.84	c

What is the value of c?

A   21.7 in.

B   21.98 in.

C   22.56 in.

D   43.96 in.

50. A cylinder has a radius of 6 cm and a height of 7 cm. A rectangular prism has a length of 9 cm, a width of 8 cm, and a height of 11 cm. What is the difference in their volumes? Use $\pi = 3.14$.

F 0.53 cm^3

G 0.72 cm^3

H 528.24 cm^3

J 660.12 cm^3

51. The scale on a blueprint is 3 in.:6 ft. The table records some results with this scale.

Blueprint	3	7	11	13
Actual	6	a	b	c

Which of the following is correct for a, b, and c?

A

a	b	c
15	22	26

B

a	b	c
15	21	39

C

a	b	c
14	22	26

D

a	b	c
14	22	39

52. The radius of a circle is 4 cm. What will the area be if radius is doubled? Use $\pi = 3.14$.

F 20.96 in.^{2}

G 50.24 in.^{2}

H 200.96 in.^{2}

J 2,009.6 in.^{2}

53. Which of the following statements is true if the only information you have is the measures of the 3 angles of a triangle?

A A unique triangle can be formed.

B More than one triangle can be formed.

C No triangles can be formed.

D Exactly two triangles can be formed.

54. The scale in the drawing of a rectangular room is 2 in.:4 ft. In the drawing, the rectangle is 5 in. by 13 in. What are the dimensions and area of the actual room?

F The room is 10 ft by 13 ft, and the area is 130 ft^2.

G The room is 10 ft by 26 ft, and the area is 260 ft^2.

H The room is 5 ft by 13 ft, and the area is 65 ft^2.

J The room is 5 ft by 26 ft, and the area is 130 ft^2.

55. Look at the parallelogram below.

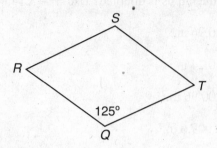

What is the measure of each acute angle?

A   55°

B   65°

C   110°

D   125°

56. What solid has only one cross section, and what is the cross section?

F   sphere, oval

G   sphere, circle

H   cube, square

J   rectangular prism, rectangle

57. A sidewalk is 2 feet wide. It surrounds a circular fountain, as shown below.

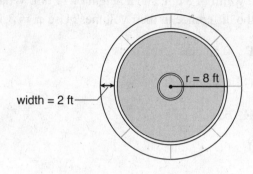

What is the area of the sidewalk?

A   113.04 ft²

B   200.96 ft²

C   314 ft²

D   514.96 ft²

58. In the scale drawing below, a rectangle is drawn on one-inch grid paper. The scale is 1 in.:4 ft.

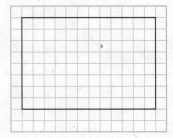

Which is the correct grid for a scale of 1 in.:8 ft?

F

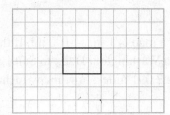

G

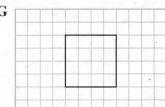

H

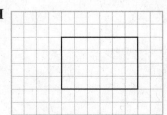

J

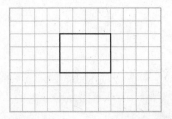

59. Pablo has 12 cubic inches of candle wax. He has a mold for a square pyramid with side measurements of 3 inches and a height of 15 inches. How much more candle wax does he need?

A 10.5 in.³

B 22 in.³

C 33 in.³

D 45 in.³

60. In the figure below, the measure of one angle is given.

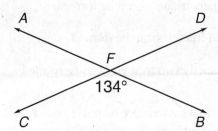

Which of the following gives the measure of the three remaining angles?

F

Angle	∠AFD	∠AFC	∠DFB
Measure	134	46	46

G

Angle	∠AFD	∠AFC	∠DFB
Measure	134	40	40

H

Angle	∠AFD	∠AFC	∠DFB
Measure	153	27	27

J

Angle	∠AFD	∠AFC	∠DFB
Measure	134	50	46

61. What is the surface area of a rectangular prism that is 32 cm long, 10 cm wide, and 7 cm high?

A 49 cm²

B 614 cm²

C 1,228 cm²

D 2,240 cm²

62. You are given angle measures of a triangle of 30°, 45°, and 60°. Which of the following is true?

F A unique triangle can be formed.

G Many triangles can be formed.

H No triangles can be formed.

J Exactly two triangles can be formed.

63. Jason draws a treasure map. He uses a scale of 2 cm = $\frac{1}{2}$ km. The actual distance from the tree to the treasure is 0.75 km. What is the distance on the map?

A 0.1875 cm

B 0.25 cm

C 1.875 cm

D 3 cm

64. Look at the figure below.

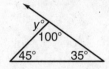

What is the measure of ∠y?

F 45°

G 35°

H 80°

J 100°

65. The scale on a map is 1 in. = 100 mi. If the distance from Washington, D.C., to Salt Lake City, Utah, is 2,091 miles, how many inches is it on the map?

A 19.91 in.

B 2.091 in.

C 21 in.

D Not Here

Geometry
Higher Scores on Math, Grade 7

66. Look at the figure below.

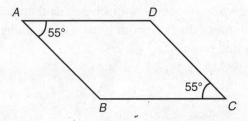

Which equation will give the measure of ∠ABC?

F $a = 180 - 2(55)$

G $a = \dfrac{360 - 2(55)}{4}$

H $a = 90 + 2(55)$

J $a = \dfrac{360 - 2(55)}{2}$

67. Look at the figure below.

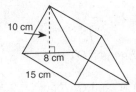

What is the volume of the prism?

A 300 cm³

B 440 cm³

C 600 cm³

D 1,200 cm³

68. The surface area of a cube is 3.84 m². What is the length of each edge of the cube?

F 0.64 m

G 0.8 m

H 0.96 m

J 23.04 m

69. Which statement is true about the angles of a trapezoid?

A Opposite angles are always supplementary.

B The sum of the measures is 360°.

C Adjacent angles are equal.

D Opposite angles are complementary.

70. Look at the figure below.

Which equation will give the measure of ∠y?

F $y = 42 + 48 - 180$

G $y = 360 - (90 + 48)$

H $y = 360 - (42 + 90 + 48)$

J $y = 180 - 48$

71. A circle with a radius of 3.5 inches is inscribed in a square. When the circle is cut out, what is the area of the pieces of the square that remain? Use $\pi = 3.14$.

A 10.54 in.²

B 27.02 in.²

C 38.47 in.²

D 49 in.²

72. Look at the figure below.

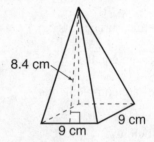

8.4 cm
9 cm
9 cm

What is the surface area of this pyramid?

F 151.2 cm²

G 232.2 cm²

H 302.4 cm²

J 378 cm²

73. The top of a plant stand is a semicircle. The straight part of the top is 20 inches long. What is the area of the top of the plant stand? Use $\pi = 3.14$.

A 157 in.²

B 200 in.²

C 314 in.²

D 419 in.²

74. A rectangular prism is 4 in. × 6 in. × 8 in. Another rectangular prism has dimensions that are twice as long. How much greater than the volume of the first prism is the volume of the second prism?

F 2 times

G 4 times

H 6 times

J 8 times

75. Look at the right triangle with measures shown below.

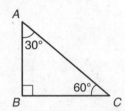

A
30°
60°
B   C

Which of the following is NOT true?

A Angles *ABC*, *BCA*, and *CAB* are supplementary.

B Angles *BCA* and *CAB* are complementary.

C Angles *BCA*, *CAB*, and *ABC* are complementary.

D Angle *B* measures 90°.

Statistics and Probability

Modeled Instruction

DIRECTIONS: Read each question and choose the best answer. Use the answer sheet provided at the end of the workbook to record your answers. If the correct answer is not available, mark the letter for "Not Here."

1. Amy wants to know the favorite supermarket of the adults in her hometown. Which is the best group to provide a random sample?

   A the members of the local women's club

   B the people coming out of a grocery store

   C every fifth person leaving a mall on a particular day

   D every tenth person entering a grocery store

   Hint

   From which group will Amy get the best and most unbiased results?

2. A coach collects data on the height of the players on the basketball teams. He finds that the results have a low mean absolute deviation (MAD). Which dot plot could represent these data?

   F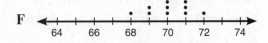

   G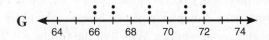

   H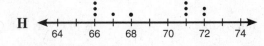

   J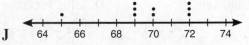

   Hint

   A low MAD means dots are clustered.

3. A number cube has numbers from 1 to 6. You toss the cube, and it lands on the number 5. Which best describes the probability of the event?

   A impossible

   B unlikely

   C as likely as not

   D certain

   Hint

   Write the probability as a fraction and see where it falls between 0 and 1.

4. At a pizza parlor, Darnell has a choice of pizza toppings and sizes. The topping choices are pineapple, onions, and mushrooms. The size choices are large and giant. Which tree diagram shows the number of possible pizza combinations that Darnell can order?

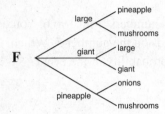

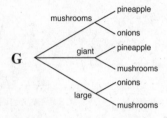

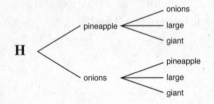

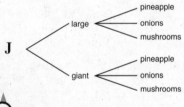

Hint

Track the various choices through the tree diagrams.

5. How far the data are spread out from the mean is a measure of —

A random sampling

B population

C mean absolute deviation

D multiple samples

Hint

Consider the definitions of each of the choices.

6. Each locker in the health club has a lock with a randomly assigned three-digit code. The code uses the digits 5, 7, and 9. Any of the numbers can be repeated. Which of the following represents the sample space?

F 18   H 36

G 27   J 54

Hint

Write down the various possibilities of combinations of the numbers 5, 7, and 9.

7. A drawer has 7 pairs of black socks and 1 pair of blue socks. You pick a pair of black socks from the drawer at random. Which of the following best describes the event?

A impossible   C as likely as not

B unlikely   D almost certain

Hint

Which color has more pairs of socks, black or blue?

8. A random sample of a shipment of picture frames shows that 15 out of every 75 have broken glass. What proportion could help find the number of picture frames with broken glass in a shipment of 800?

F $\frac{15}{75} = \frac{x}{800}$

G $\frac{15}{75} = \frac{800}{x}$

H $\frac{15}{800} = \frac{x}{75}$

J $\frac{800}{75} = \frac{15}{x}$

 Hint

The ratios in the proportion should compare like quantities.

9. Ana has a box of different-colored balls. She removes one ball and records the color. She then puts the ball back in the box. She repeats this process several times and records the results in the table below.

Color	Frequency
Black	20
White	15
Purple	18
Orange	22

What is the experimental probability of selecting a purple ball?

A 0.24   C 0.29

B 0.26   D 0.33

 Hint

Probability is found by the ratio of the number of events to the total of the possible events.

10. A shipment to a warehouse consists of 4,000 DVDs. The receiving clerk chooses the top 3 DVDs and finds that none of the cases are cracked. Can she assume that there are no defective DVD cases in the entire shipment? Why or why not?

F Yes, 3 is a representative random sample.

G No, 3 is a biased sample.

H Yes, she is biased.

J No, her sample is not random and is too small.

 Hint

What would be a reasonable sample to choose for 4,000 DVDs?

11. A coin is flipped 12 times. Which experimental probability is most consistent with the theoretical probability?

A 2 heads and 10 tails

B 4 heads and 8 tails

C 6 heads and 6 tails

D 8 heads and 4 tails

 Hint

Think about the theoretical probability of flipping a coin. What is the chance that the coin will land on heads? What about the next time the coin is flipped?

12. Tanya has 3 red hats and 2 blue hats. If she picks one hat at random 100 times, how many times will she pick a red hat?

F 0.4   **H** 40

G 0.6   **J** 60

Hint

Find the probability for one test and multiply by 100.

13. Javier is evaluating the data that show how many years he has been friends with some of his classmates. He says the mean is 7.2 and the MAD is 4. Tony is looking at the same data for his classmates. His mean is 5.2, and his MAD is 2.

Which of the following can be concluded from these data?

A Javier's friendships have lasted longer.

B Tony's friendships have lasted longer.

C Javier's friendships lasted the same length of time as Tony's.

D Javier is no longer making friends.

Hint

What do mean and MAD tell about the data?

14. Julian and his friends average their test scores and find that the average is 90. The teacher announces that the average of the test scores in her classes is 80. Why are the averages so different?

F The teacher made a mistake in calculating the average.

G Julian and his friends are not representative of all students in the class.

H Julian made a mistake in calculating the average.

J The sample Julian used was not large enough to make an accurate prediction.

Hint

Is the sample consisting of Julian and his friends a sufficient sample?

15. The table below represents the sums when 2 number cubes are tossed.

	1	2	3	4	5	6
1	2	3	4	5	6	7
2	3	4	5	6	7	8
3	4	5	6	7	8	9
4	5	6	7	8	9	10
5	6	7	8	9	10	11
6	7	8	9	10	11	12

What is the probability that the sum will be less than 7 when a number cube is tossed?

A $\frac{1}{6}$ **B** $\frac{5}{12}$ **C** $\frac{1}{2}$ **D** $\frac{7}{2}$

Hint

Probability is found by the ratio of the number of events to the total of the possible events.

16. Vo collects data on the number of magazines sold by the students in her class.

Magazines Sold
5 4 3 6 4 5 5 2 3 4

What are the mean and MAD for these data?

F   Mean = 0.92, and MAD = 4.1.

G   Mean = 4.1, and MAD = 0.92.

H   Mean = 4.1, and MAD = 4.1.

J   Mean = 0.92, and MAD = 0.92.

Hint

Mean is the sum of the data divided by the total number. MAD is the mean of the absolute values of the data from the mean.

17. Two teachers have calculated the mean and MAD for a series of test scores of their final exams. Ms. Hoang's mean is 90, and her MAD is 1. Mr. Smith's mean is 85, and his MAD is 4. How would you expect the dot plots of the data sets to compare with each other?

A   Mr. Smith's data will be farther to the right and less spread out than Ms. Hoang's.

B   Ms. Hoang's data will be farther to the right and less spread out than Mr. Smith's.

C   Mr. Smith's data will be farther to the left and less spread out than Ms. Hoang's.

D   Ms. Hoang's data will be farther to the left and clustered.

Hint

Numbers on a number line get larger as you move to the right. A low MAD means the dots will be clustered.

18. The following table comes from a probability simulation. The number 1 measures the outcome.

Trial	Random Numbers	Events
1	1 0 7 0 6	1
2	3 6 6 0 0	0
3	1 2 0 3 1	2
4	8 5 7 3 5	0
5	3 8 0 7 3	0
6	8 1 1 5 7	2
7	7 8 6 6 2	0
8	3 2 7 3 2	0
9	9 7 0 7 9	0
10	3 0 5 9 6	0

What is the experimental probability of getting at least one 1 in a trial?

F   0.06   **G**   0.1   **H**   0.3   **J**   0.5

Hint

Count the number of times 1 appears in the random numbers.

19. A spinner is divided into 2 parts. May spins the spinner 3 times. After she spins, she creates the tree diagram below.

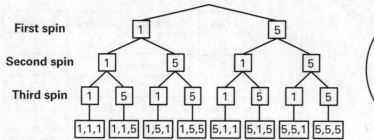
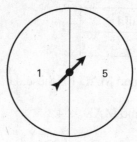

First spin · Second spin · Third spin

1,1,1 1,1,5 1,5,1 1,5,5 5,1,1 5,1,5 5,5,1 5,5,5

What is the probability of spinning 2 fives in the 3 attempts?

A $\frac{3}{8}$ 　　　　 B $\frac{1}{2}$ 　　　　 C $\frac{8}{3}$ 　　　　 D Not Here

Hint

Probability is found by the ratio of the number of events to the total of the possible events.

20. The probability of an event happening is $\frac{7}{8}$. About how many times will the event occur in 250 trials?

F 31 　　　　 G 218 　　　　 H 285 　　　　 J Not Here

Hint

Probability is found by the ratio of the number of events to the total of the possible events.

21. What is the theoretical probability of getting a 6 when tossing a number cube one time?

A 12.5% 　　　　 B 16.7% 　　　　 C 20% 　　　　 D 25%

Hint

Probability is found by the ratio of the number of events to the total of the possible events.

22. A sample in which every person, object, or event has an equal chance at being selected is called a —

F population   **G** sample   **H** random sample   **J** biased sample

 Hint

Think about the meaning of "equal chance."

---

23. Ruth has a jar of fruit candies. She removes one piece at random, records the flavor, and puts it back. She repeats the process many times and records the results in the table below.

Flavor	Frequency
Strawberry	18
Orange	40
Watermelon	37
Grape	20
Lemon	35

What is the experimental probability of each flavor?

A

Strawberry	Orange	Watermelon	Grape	Lemon
$\frac{37}{150}$	$\frac{4}{15}$	$\frac{3}{25}$	$\frac{2}{15}$	$\frac{7}{30}$

B

Strawberry	Orange	Watermelon	Grape	Lemon
$\frac{4}{15}$	$\frac{3}{25}$	$\frac{2}{15}$	$\frac{7}{30}$	$\frac{37}{150}$

C

Strawberry	Orange	Watermelon	Grape	Lemon
$\frac{3}{25}$	$\frac{4}{15}$	$\frac{7}{30}$	$\frac{2}{15}$	$\frac{37}{150}$

D

Strawberry	Orange	Watermelon	Grape	Lemon
$\frac{3}{25}$	$\frac{4}{15}$	$\frac{37}{150}$	$\frac{2}{15}$	$\frac{7}{30}$

 Hint

Probability is found by the ratio of the number of events to the total of the possible events.

24. A transportation consultant did a random sample of airline arrivals and found that 15 out of 100 arrivals were late. Based on these results, how many late arrivals would she expect to find in 64,000 flights?

F 42

G 640

H 4,266

J 9,600

Hint

The ratio and proportion used to solve this problem should compare like quantities.

25. Two people living in different parts of the world calculate the mean and MAD of their average temperatures. Both have the same mean, but the MAD numbers are very different, one being 5.3 and the other 25.7. What can you infer from these data?

A The MAD of 25.7 indicates a wide spread between the low and high temperatures.

B The MAD of 5.3 indicates a wide spread between the high and low temperatures.

C The MAD of 5.3 has a mean of 76°.

D The MAD of 6.6 has a mean of 100°.

Hint

Think about what a low MAD tells about the data.

Statistics and Probability

Independent Practice

DIRECTIONS: Read each question and choose the best answer. Use the answer sheet provided at the end of the workbook to record your answers. If the correct answer is not available, mark the letter for "Not Here."

26. A baseball team has 9 boys and 4 girls. Each week the coach chooses one of them to be the umpire. What is the probability the coach will choose a girl?

    F $\frac{4}{13}$

    G $\frac{4}{9}$

    H $\frac{9}{13}$

    J 1

27. The graphs represent data about test scores. Which dot plot shows the lowest mean absolute deviation?

    A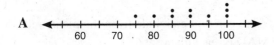

    B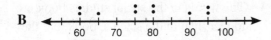

    C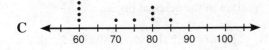

    D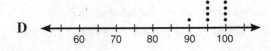

28. When information is being gathered about a group, the entire group of objects, individuals, or events is called a —

    F population

    G sample

    H biased sample

    J random sample

29. You toss a number cube 2,000 times. Which of the following is the best prediction of the number of times you will get a 1 or a 3?

    A 33

    B 333

    C 666

    D 1,333

30. The probability of an event happening is 0.008. Which statement best describes the probability of this event?

    F The event is likely to happen.

    G The event is not likely to happen.

    H The event is neither likely nor not likely to happen.

    J The event is not possible.

31. Which of the following terms is described by this formula?

$$P\,(\text{event}) = \frac{\text{number of ways the event can occur}}{\text{total number of equally likely outcomes}}$$

A predictive probability

B theoretical probability

C experimental probability

D probability complement

32. Which event is certain to happen?

F You have six spaces on a spinner, and each one contains a star. You land on a star.

G You have a bag of black marbles. You randomly pull out a red marble.

H You toss two number cubes and find the sum. The sum is an even number.

J You have a spinner with 4 spaces. Three spaces are black and one is red. You land on a black space.

33. A spinner has 5 sections, each a different color. What is the complement of the probability that the spinner will stop on one specific color?

A $1 + \frac{1}{5}$

B $1 - \frac{1}{5}$

C $1 - \frac{4}{5}$

D $1 + \frac{4}{5}$

34. Mr. Chou is redecorating his office. He has a choice of 4 colors of paint, 3 kinds of window coverings, and 2 colors of carpet. How many different combinations of paint, window coverings, and carpet does he have?

F 9

G 12

H 14

J 24

35. The lengths of a random selection of words in a science book and in a social studies book are listed below.

Science Book
6 8 6 4 8 3 3 7 5 7 5 6 2 6 7

Social Studies Book
2 4 5 4 6 1 3 4 5 6 2 1 5 6 3

What can you conclude from the mean and MAD of each data set?

A The words in the social studies book are longer than in the science book, but the variation in the social studies book is greater than in the science book.

B The words in the social studies book are shorter than in the science book, and the variation in the social studies book is significantly greater than in the science book.

C The words in the science book are longer than those in the social studies book, but the variation between the word lengths in the two books is virtually the same.

D The word lengths in the two books are virtually the same, but the lengths vary more in the social studies book.

36. The following data are given: 12, 9, 16, 23, 30, 9, 6, 15, 18, and 23. Which of the following shows the mean and MAD for these data?

F   Mean = 16.1, and MAD = 16.1.

G   Mean = 16.1, and MAD = 5.92.

H   Mean = 5.92, and MAD = 5.92.

J   Mean = 5.92, and MAD = 16.1.

37. Look at the table below.

	Mean	MAD
Team A	18.6	4
Team B	12	1

Which statement CANNOT be made about these data?

A   On a dot plot, Team A will be farther to the right, and the dots will be spread out.

B   On a dot plot, Team B will be farther to the left, and the dots will be clustered.

C   The mean for Team A was determined from more scores than the mean for Team B.

D   Not Here

38. In a standard deck of cards, the probability of choosing a card at random and getting an 8 is $\frac{1}{13}$. What is the probability of NOT getting an 8?

F $\frac{1}{13}$

G $\frac{1}{4}$

H $\frac{8}{14}$

J $\frac{12}{13}$

39. A drawer contains 6 black socks and 8 white socks. If Kara draws 2 socks out of the drawer in the dark, what is the probability that both will be white?

A $\frac{4}{13}$

B $\frac{2}{7}$

C $\frac{1}{4}$

D $\frac{1}{7}$

40. Two families have 8 people each. The ages of the family members are listed in the tables below.

Ages of Family 1
36 6 43 10 17 4 9 13

Ages of Family 2
26 3 10 4 8 36 7 10

Which of the following statements is correct for the variability of the ages of the two families?

F   The variability is the same because the MADs are equal.

G   The variability for Family 1 is greater because the mean is greater.

H   The variability for Family 1 is greater because the MAD is greater.

J   The variability for Family 2 is greater because the MAD is greater.

41. Prestige Builders has a new development of homes. There are 5 different floor plans, 4 exterior colors, and an option of either a 2-car or a 3-car garage. How many choices are there for each home?

A 20

B 34

C 40

D 60

42. A shipment to a warehouse consists of 5,000 books. A manager chooses to inspect 100 books at random. She finds that 15 books have pages upside down. How many books in the shipment are likely to have this problem?

F 3

G 233

H 333

J 750

43. Celina is going through her closet. She sees that she has 4 different colors of skirts, 4 different colors of blouses, and 3 different colors of jackets. How many combinations can she make?

A 11

B 28

C 48

D 60

44. A teacher randomly reads 5 written reports from the 125 she has to grade. She finds that 3 reports did not follow the correct style. At this same rate, how many of the 125 can she expect to not follow the correct style?

F 25

G 40

H 41

J 75

45. If you toss two coins, how many times would you expect to get two heads in 1,000 tries?

A 250

B 500

C 750

D Not Here

46. At one of the game booths at the county fair, you have a choice of using Spinner A or Spinner B. If you land on a section marked with an "X", you win a prize.

Spinner A   Spinner B

 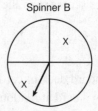

Which spinner should you choose and why?

F Spinner A, because the probability is $\frac{1}{3}$.

G Spinner B, because the probability is $\frac{1}{2}$.

H Spinner A, because it has a higher probability.

J Spinner B, because the probability and its complement equal 1.

47. Look at the dot plot below.

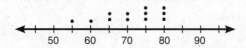

Which of the following is a list of the data shown in the dot plot?

A 55, 60, 65, 70, 75, 80, 65, 70, 80, 80

B 50, 60, 70, 80, 55, 65, 70, 75, 75, 80, 80

C 55, 60, 65, 70, 70, 75, 75, 75, 80, 80, 80

D 55, 60, 65, 65, 70, 70, 75, 75, 75, 80, 80, 80

48. The school cook wants to find out the favorite dessert of middle school students. Which of the following is the correct population to sample?

F boys basketball team members

G girls in gym class

H all students entering the cafeteria on a particular day

J students in Mr. Medrano's seventh grade class

49. Myra tosses two number cubes and adds the numbers together. What is the probability that the sum will be an even number?

A $\frac{4}{36}$

B $\frac{9}{36}$

C $\frac{18}{36}$

D $\frac{36}{36}$

50. Which of the following is a random sample in a survey to determine the most common eye color of students in the high school?

F random students entering the freshman class

G random students leaving the school on two afternoons during the week

H random students eating in the cafeteria on Monday

J random students driving to school

51. The probability of an event happening is $\frac{1}{4}$. If you recreate the event 500 times, about how many times will this event happen?

A 100

B 125

C 375

D 2,000

52. Angela tosses a number cube onto a black and red checkerboard. What is the probability that it will land with a value greater than 2 and on a red square?

F $\frac{1}{3}$

G $\frac{5}{12}$

H $\frac{7}{6}$

J $\frac{5}{3}$

53. Micah draws a marble at random from a basket. He records the color and puts the marble back. He repeats this experiment several times and records the results in the table below.

Color	Frequency
Black	8
White	15
Clear	7
Yellow	5

What is the experimental probability of choosing a clear marble?

A $\frac{1}{7}$

B $\frac{1}{5}$

C $\frac{8}{35}$

D $\frac{3}{7}$

54. The probability of an event that "is as likely as not" to happen can be expressed by which of the following percents?

F 25%

G 50%

H 75%

J 100%

55. A pilot counted the number of empty seats on some recent flights. His results are shown in the table below.

Empty Seats
5 1 8 9 4 9

Which statement best describes what you can conclude from the data?

A The mean is 2.67, and the MAD is 6.

B The mean is 6, and the MAD is 2.67.

C There is a great deal of variability among the 6 flights.

D The number of empty seats on all flights is almost the same.

56. A box contains 7 black marbles and 9 white marbles. If Kendra draws 2 marbles at random out of the box and does not return them to the box, what is the complement of the probability that both are black?

F $\frac{1}{49}$

G $\frac{48}{49}$

H $\frac{33}{40}$

J $\frac{7}{40}$

57. Based on a random sample during the prior week, a manager of a fast-food restaurant estimates that each day, out of 350 people, 50 will order a salad. What ratio of people will order a salad each day?

A $\frac{1}{70}$

B $\frac{1}{7}$

C $\frac{6}{7}$

D $\frac{7}{7}$

58. The theoretical probability of an event happening is 75%. After a series of actual trials, the experimental probability comes out to 50%. Which of the following most likely explains the reason for the difference?

F The experiment was designed wrong.

G The number of trials in the experiment was too small.

H The number of trials in the experiment was too large.

J The theoretical probability was calculated incorrectly.

59. Paula wants to know the type of music the band members at the middle school prefer to play. Whom should she survey?

A the students in the cafeteria

B the students in Mrs. Patel's music class

C the students in the school band

D the students in the school

60. Bo is fixing computers. He knows that of the 12 computers he has, there are 4 with bad motherboards and 6 with failed power supplies. What is the probability that the first computer he analyzes has both issues?

F 0.016

G 0.1667

H 1.16

J 1.666

61. Each letter in EXPERIMENTAL is written on a separate piece of paper and put into a bag. You randomly draw a piece of paper from the bag. What is the probability that you will draw an *E?*

A 0.69%

B 1.3%

C 8.3%

D 25%

62. Which of the following can be used to calculate the MAD of a set of data?

F Find the mean. Then find the absolute value of each number from the mean. Then find the mean of these numbers.

G Find the mean. Then find the absolute value of each number from the mean and subtract each number from the mean.

H Find the mean of the data set. This will also be the MAD.

J Add together the numbers in the data set and then find the difference between each number and the sum you just found. Find the mean of these differences.

63. You want to know which TV channel most people in your neighborhood watch during prime time. How would you get a random sample?

    A Survey people in the phone directory.

    B Survey people who pass by a central location in your neighborhood.

    C Survey the people who voted in the last election.

    D Survey people going inside the neighborhood cell-phone store.

64. Which of the following is NOT the probability of getting a 2 on a number cube?

    F $\frac{1}{6}$

    G 1.67%

    H one out of 6

    J 0.1666…

65. The Salazar family has a combination lock on the front door. Family members can use any combination of the numbers 3, 4, and 5 in their code. Any of the numbers can be repeated. What is the probability that they will choose a number with 5 as the three digits?

    A $\frac{1}{81}$

    B $\frac{2}{27}$

    C $\frac{1}{9}$

    D Not Here

66. Which of the following best describes that an event "is likely" to happen?

    F 0.25

    G 0.50

    H 0.75

    J 1.0

67. The planners of the concert need to know how many people bought reserved seats in the previous five years. The results appear in the table below.

Reserved Seats
40 18 86 36 18

    What is the best conclusion that can be made from these data?

    A Two numbers fall above the mean.

    B There is not a lot of variability among the data.

    C The mean is 18.72.

    D The MAD is 39.6.

68. A department store receives a shipment of 500 cartons of glasses. Out of a random sample of 50 cartons, 10 cartons contained broken glasses. How many cartons in the entire shipment are expected to contain broken glasses?

F 5

G 10

H 100

J 250

69. Georgina watches the cashier scan 7 items in her shopping cart. The prices appear in the table below.

Prices
89 85 84 85 78 75 77

What is the best conclusion you can make for these data based on the mean and MAD?

A The MAD of 4.4 indicates only slight variation in the prices.

B The MAD of 81.86 indicates a great deal of variety in the prices.

C The mean is 87.85.

D Not Here

70. Ari is developing a probability simulation and has created the table below. He determines that the number 3 will measure his outcome.

Trial	Random Numbers	Events
1	6 1 1 6 7	0
2	4 5 1 4 5	0
3	4 4 4 8 2	0
4	6 1 1 0 4	0
5	4 2 3 4 6	1
6	4 3 4 1 3	2
7	9 1 4 8 0	0
8	1 1 3 7 0	1
9	3 6 7 3 0	2
10	8 3 5 9 8	1

What is the experimental probability of getting at least one 3 in a trial?

F 0.08

G 0.1

H 0.5

J 0.7

71. Olivia conducts an experiment and gets 4 positive results out of 5 trials. What is the experimental probability of a positive result?

A $\frac{1}{5}$

B 60%

C 80%

D $\frac{5}{4}$

72. When David gets dressed in the morning, his closet is dark. His closet contains 2 pairs of black shoes and 1 pair of brown shoes. Each day he pulls out one pair of shoes at random. How many times in the month of April should he expect to pull out a black pair of shoes?

F 0

G 10

H 20

J 30

73. What is the probability of choosing an *N* or an *A* at random from pieces of paper, each containing a letter from the word *ENGAGEMENT*?

A $\frac{1}{50}$

B $\frac{3}{100}$

C $\frac{1}{10}$

D $\frac{3}{10}$

74. If you roll a number cube 150 times, about how many times do you expect to roll a 2 or a 4?

F 25

G 37

H 50

J 75

75. A random sample of cell phones shows that 3 out of every 15 are shipped with the wrong car charger. Which proportion could help you find the number of phones with the wrong car charger out of a shipment of 750 phones?

A $\frac{1}{5} = \frac{x}{750}$

B $\frac{1}{5} = \frac{750}{x}$

C $\frac{5}{1} = \frac{x}{750}$

D $\frac{3}{15} = \frac{750}{x}$

Name _____   Date _____

Practice Test A

DIRECTIONS: Read each question and choose the best answer. Use the answer sheet provided at the end of the workbook to record your answers. If the correct answer is not available, mark the letter for "Not Here."

1. Jean raises $1,572.50 for her favorite charity. Her expenses are $500.75. Richard raises $3,275.50 for his favorite charity. His expenses are $1,001.36. Who gives more to charity and by how much?

   A Jean by $1,202.39

   B Richard by $1,202.39

   C Jean by $1,700.25

   D Richard by $1,700.25

2. Two pools are being filled with water. Pool A is filled at the rate of 3 gallons every $\frac{1}{4}$ hour. Pool B is filled at a rate of 4 gallons every $\frac{1}{2}$ hour. Which expression is correct for the pool that is filling faster?

   F $\frac{3}{\frac{1}{4}}$

   G $3 \times \frac{1}{4}$

   H $\frac{4}{\frac{1}{2}}$

   J $4 \div 3$

3. In a retail setting, merchandise is very often sold for $1\frac{1}{2}$ times its cost. If the retailer pays $175.00 for men's suits, what is the selling price?

   A $112.50

   B $196.87

   C $218.00

   D $262.50

4. Simplify the expression $3(x + 5) + 4(x - 3)$.

   F $7x + 27$

   G $-x + 12$

   H $7x + 3$

   J $7x - 3$

5. In the figure below, the measurement of two angles is given.

   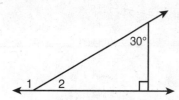

   Which of the following gives the measures of $\angle 1$ and $\angle 2$?

   A $\angle 1 = 120°$, and $\angle 2 = 60°$.

   B $\angle 1 = 134°$, and $\angle 2 = 46°$.

   C $\angle 1 = 110°$, and $\angle 2 = 90°$.

   D $\angle 1 = 60°$, and $\angle 2 = 30°$.

6. Mr. Gupta is redecorating his office. He has a choice of 3 colors of paint, 2 kinds of window coverings, and 2 colors of carpet. Which of the following is the correct tree diagram?

F
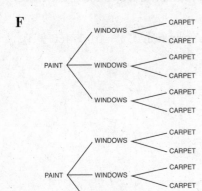

G
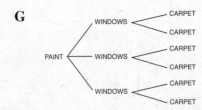

H
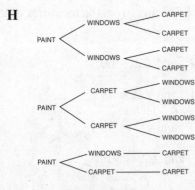

J
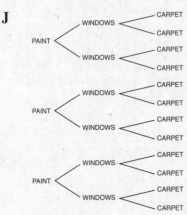

7. Nathan has $365.72 in his checking account. He deposits $200.00. During the month, he withdraws $75.30 four times. What is his balance at the end of the month?

  A $64.52

  B $264.52

  C $490.42

  D $565.72

8. The ratio of the number of men to women teachers in the school is $\frac{3}{7}$. There are 32 teachers in the school. Which equation shows how to find the number of teachers who are men?

  F $3x = 224$

  G $10x = 32$

  H $10x = 96$

  J $3x = 32$

9. A booth at the flea market is $100.00 for the weekend, plus 10% commission on sales. If sales are $50.00, how much does the booth cost?

  A $60.00

  B $105.00

  C $140.00

  D $150.00

10. Find the value of the expression $\dfrac{3\frac{1}{2} + 5\frac{1}{4} - 7\frac{3}{8}}{2\frac{1}{3}}$.

   F -0.589

   G 0.589

   H 6.91

   J 15.02

11. The length of a side of the base of a square pyramid is 10 cm. The height of the pyramid is 15.2 cm. What is the volume?

   A 152 cm^3

   B 304 cm^3

   C 506.7 cm^3

   D $2,310.4 \text{ cm}^3$

12. Is -30.75 a rational number? Which of the following is the best reason why or why not?

   F   Yes, it can be written as $-30\frac{3}{4}$.

   G   Yes, it can be written as $30\frac{3}{4}$.

   H   No, it is less than 0.

   J   No, its additive inverse is a positive number.

13. Mathew sells half the books in his library. After he does this, he buys 6 more books. Now he has 102 books. How many books did he have to start with?

   A   106

   B   192

   C   198

   D   216

14. Which of the following is a random sample to determine the average age of the spectators at a football game?

   F   Ask a random number of people purchasing tickets.

   G   Ask a random number of people who are members of the football team.

   H   Ask 10 people at random as they enter the stadium.

   J   Ask every 5th person who enters or leaves the football stadium.

15. The furniture store sells dining room tables and chairs. Single chairs for a particular table sell for $75.00 each. The cost for 4 chairs when the customer purchases the entire set is $200.00. What is the percent savings on the 4-chair set rounded to the nearest whole percent?

   A   25%

   B   33%

   C   50%

   D   66%

16. What is the constant of proportionality shown in this graph?

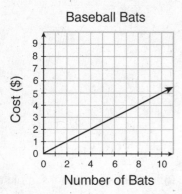

Baseball Bats

F   0

G $\frac{1}{2}$

H   1

J   2

17. Beth is making the minimum wage of $7.25 per hour. Her boss promises her a raise of 5%. How much more per week will she make if she works a 37.5-hour week?

A $1.87

B $13.59

C $271.87

D $285.46

18. The perimeter of a building is 320 meters. The length of the building is 100 meters. What is the width?

F   60 m

G   100 m

H   120 m

J   200 m

19. What is the surface area of a rectangular prism with measurements 10 in. × 15 in. × 9 in.?

A   48 in.²

B   375 in.²

C   750 in.²

D   1,350 in.²

20. Look at the graph.

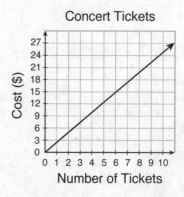

Concert Tickets

Which of the following is a true statement?

F   The unit rate is 3.

G   The point (6, 15) is on the graph.

H   The point (5, 12) is on the graph.

J   The constant of proportionality is 3.

21. Look at the parallelogram below.

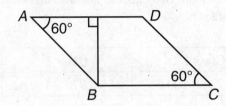

Which equation gives the measure of $\angle ABC$?

A $\angle ABC = \dfrac{360 - 2(60)}{2}$

B $\angle ABC = 360 - \dfrac{2(60)}{4}$

C $\angle ABC = 180 - 2(60)$

D $\angle ABC = 90 + 2(60)$

22. A piece of material is $4\frac{1}{6}$ yards long. It is cut into four pieces of equal length. How long is each piece?

F 1.042 in.

G 1.042 yd

H 2.89 in.

J 16.666... ft

23. The table below represents the sums when 2 number cubes are tossed.

	1	2	3	4	5	6
1	2	3	4	5	6	7
2	3	4	5	6	7	8
3	4	5	6	7	8	9
4	5	6	7	8	9	10
5	6	7	8	9	10	11
6	7	8	9	10	11	12

What is the probability that the sum will be equal to or greater than 7?

A $\dfrac{1}{3}$

B $\dfrac{5}{12}$

C $\dfrac{7}{12}$

D $\dfrac{5}{6}$

24. You have a spinner with sections numbered 1 through 6. When you spin, what is the complement of the probability that you will land on a number greater than 4?

F $\dfrac{1}{3}$

G $\dfrac{2}{3}$

H $\dfrac{5}{6}$

J $\dfrac{3}{2}$

25. Jeanette has $565.25 in her checking account. She makes one deposit of $10.00 and then withdraws $45.60 seven times. What is her balance?

    A $236.05

    B $256.05

    C $347.25

    D $529.65

26. Simplify the fraction $\frac{\frac{3}{7}}{\frac{5}{8}}$.

    F $\frac{15}{56}$

    G $\frac{24}{35}$

    H $\frac{35}{24}$

    J $\frac{56}{15}$

27. The price of stock in a software company drops by $42.60 over a 16-day period. On average, how much does it drop per day?

    A $0.37

    B $2.60

    C $26.60

    D   Not Here

28. The principal is comparing a random number of test scores from two classes. The data are shown in the tables below.

Class 1	Class 2
90 86 72 60 100 85	65 70 97 86 100 82

Find the mean and MAD for each set of data. Then choose the statement that is NOT correct for the variability of the two classes.

    F   The variability of the two classes is almost the same.

    G   The variability for Class 1 is greater than for Class 2.

    H   The mean for Class 2 is greater than for Class 1.

    J   The classes are almost identical in mean and variability.

29. Jamila's cake recipe calls for $4\frac{1}{4}$ cups of flour. She cuts the recipe in half. How much flour does she use?

    A   1 cup

    B $2\frac{1}{8}$ cups

    C $2\frac{1}{4}$ cups

    D $8\frac{1}{2}$ cups

30. Look at the data table below.

Animal Weights
60 48 52 86 75 80 50

What are the mean and MAD for these data?

F Mean = 13.63, and MAD = 13.63.

G Mean = 64.43, and MAD = 64.43.

H Mean = 64.43, and MAD = 13.63.

J Mean = 13.63, and MAD = 64.43.

31. What are the unit rate (u) and constant of proportionality (c) of the data in this table?

Time (s)	2	3	4	5
Distance (mi)	24	36	48	60

A $u = 12$ and $c = 12$

B $u = 24$ and $c = 24$

C $u = 36$ and $c = 48$

D $u = 24$ and $c = 2$

32. Which of the following numbers is one solution to this inequality?

$$-4x + 64 < 242 + 3x$$

F 25.4

G -43.7

H -52.8

J -62.1

33. Look at the figure below.

What is the measure of $\angle y$?

A 42°

B 90°

C 132°

D 312°

34. The scale on a map is 1 in.:100 mi. If the distance from Chicago, Illinois, to Austin, Texas, is 1,162 miles, how far apart are the two cities on the map?

F 11 in.

G 11.5 in.

H 11.62 in.

J 12 in.

35. An equation for a proportional relationship is $y = 5x$. Which of the following gives the points that will fall on the graph?

A (3, 12), (7, 24), (9, 36)

B (2, 10), (4, 20), (7, 28)

C (3, 15), (6, 30), (8, 40)

D (0, 0), (9, 40), (1, 55)

36. The table below shows different ways a cylinder and a plane can intersect.

Intersection	Figure Formed
The plane is parallel to the bases of the cylinder.	x
The plane is not parallel and not through the bases.	y
The plane intersects both bases of the cylinder.	z

Which of the following is true of x, y, and z?

F
x	y	z
circle	oval	rectangle

G
x	y	z
oval	circle	rectangle

H
x	y	z
rectangle	oval	circle

J
x	y	z
circle	rectangle	oval

37. The scale drawing of a rectangle to represent a room is 2 in.:4 ft. In the drawing, the rectangle is 8 in. × 14 in. What are the dimensions and the area of the actual room?

A Dimensions are 8 ft × 14 ft, and area is 112 ft².

B Dimensions are 8 ft × 14 ft, and area is 44 ft².

C Dimensions are 16 ft × 28 ft, and area is 448 ft².

D Dimensions are 16 ft × 28 ft, and area is 88 ft².

38. Solve the inequality.

$$\frac{(4y)}{9} < -12$$

F $y \le -27$

G $y = -4\frac{8}{9}$

H $y < -27$

J $y > -27$

39. If you toss a number cube 300 times, about how many times do you expect to get a 2?

A 50

B 100

C 150

D 200

40. A table is being centered on a wall. The wall is 12 feet long, and the table is 5 feet long. Which equation can be used to determine how much of the wall should be on each side of the table?

F $12 - 5 \div 2 = x$

G $(12 + 5) \div 2 = x$

H $(12 - 5) \div 2 = x$

J $12 + 5 \div 2 = x$

41. An elevator moves at a constant speed of 27 feet per second. If this proportional relationship is shown on a coordinate graph, which of the following points will NOT fall on the graph?

A (0, 0)

B (1, 27)

C (2, 56)

D (3, 81)

42. Luis is developing a probability simulation and has created a table showing 10 trials. He determines that 0 will measure his outcome.

Trial	Random Numbers	Outcome
1	4 9 1 0 4	1
2	3 7 2 6 5	0
3	4 6 0 2 7	1
4	4 6 1 0 5	1
5	6 2 6 7 8	0
6	6 2 4 4 4	0
7	5 9 1 2 8	0
8	0 0 3 4 4	2
9	3 8 1 9 6	0
10	3 3 7 3 3	0

What is the experimental probability of getting at least one 0 in a trial?

F 0.03

G 0.4

H 0.5

J 0.6

43. Given the three angles of a triangle, which of the following is true?

A You can draw a unique triangle.

B You can draw more than one triangle.

C You can draw exactly 2 triangles.

D Not Here

44. A sidewalk that is 3 feet wide surrounds a circular garden with a radius of 10 feet. What is the area of the sidewalk? Use $\pi = 3.14$.

F 18.84 ft^2

G 216.66 ft^2

H 314 ft^2

J 530.66 ft^2

45. A CD player sells for $60.00. The company is offering a discount of 25% because the model is being discontinued. There is a 7% sales tax. If Sally pays with a $100.00 bill, how much change will she receive?

A $35.80

B $48.15

C $51.85

D $64.20

46. Joseph's credit limit on his credit card is $300.00. For every $100.00 above the limit, the bank charges $5.00. If his balance goes to $375.00, how much will the bank charge if it prorates the fee?

F $0

G $2.50

H $3.75

J $5.00

47. A cube and a plane intersect. Which of the following is NOT a list of possible cross sections?

A trapezoid, parallelogram, square

B rectangle, trapezoid, square

C triangle, rectangle, circle

D triangle, trapezoid, parallelogram

48. Which table shows a proportional relationship?

F

1	2	3	4
11	22	33	45

G

5	6	8	10
25	26	28	29

H

5	6	7	8
10	12	14	18

J

1	2	3	4
5	10	15	20

49. The diameter of a round table is 54 inches. What are the circumference and area of the table? Use $\pi = 3.14$.

A

Circumference	Area
14 ft	15 ft^2

B

Circumference	Area
2,2890.06 ft	169.56 in.^{2}

C

Circumference	Area
15 ft^2	14 ft^2

D

Circumference	Area
169.56 in.	2,289.06 in.^{2}

50. Jamil has $175.00 to spend on bats and balls for the team. All the bats are the same price, and all the balls are the same price. The balls he wants total $85.00. Which expression indicates how much he can spend on bats?

F $x \leq 90$

G $x \geq 90$

H $2x \leq 90$

J $2x \geq 90$

51. Which of the following is NOT true for the equation $x = -4,875 + 9,633$?

A The sum will be a positive number.

B The sum will be 4,758.

C The sum will be a negative number.

D The equation is the same as $x = 9,633 - 4,875$.

52. New Homes Builders has a new development of homes. There are 4 different floor plans, 4 exterior colors, 3 roof colors, and 2 garage sizes that new buyers can choose. How many choices are there for one home?

F 13

G 24

H 48

J 96

53. A shipment to a warehouse consists of 300 laptop computers. The receiving clerk looks at the top 5 laptops in the first shipping container and finds there are no defects. Can the clerk assume the shipment is perfect? Why or why not?

A No, 5 from the first box is not a good random sample.

B Yes, 5 from the first box is a good random sample.

C Yes, the sample is not biased.

D No, 5 out of 300 is too small a sample.

54. Reggie sells books. Hardcover books sell for $16.50. Paperback books sell for $7.95. He keeps 30% of his sales. If he sells 5 hardcover books and 11 paperback books, how much does he earn?

F $50.99

G $82.50

H $87.45

J $122.47

55. Laurel picks a marble from a box without looking. She records the color and puts the marble back in the box. She repeats the experiment several times and records the results in the table below.

Color	Frequency
Striped	5
Spotted	8
Clear	3
Yellow	6
Orange	2

What is the experimental probability of choosing a spotted marble?

A $\frac{5}{24}$

B $\frac{1}{4}$

C $\frac{1}{3}$

D $\frac{2}{3}$

56. A seventh grade class has 15 boys and 10 girls. Each week the teacher chooses someone to be the class leader for the week. What is the probability that the teacher will choose a girl?

F $\dfrac{1}{5}$

G $\dfrac{2}{5}$

H $\dfrac{3}{5}$

J $\dfrac{2}{3}$

57. John's business had sales in August of $3,256.00. In the same month, his expenses were $4,000.00. What is his profit for the month?

A $-$7,256.00

B $-$744.00

C $744.00

D $7,256.00

58. Which of these sets of ordered pairs does NOT form a proportional relationship?

F (0, 0), (1, 5), (2, 6), (3, 8)

G (0, 0), (1, 3), (2, 6), (3, 9)

H (0, 0), (2, 4), (3, 6), (4, 8)

J (0, 0), (1, 5), (2, 10), (3, 15)

59. The temperature in El Paso, Texas, on Friday was 30°C. Over the weekend, the temperature changed by -17°C. What was the temperature on Monday morning?

A -13°C

B 13°C

C 77°C

D Not Here

60. Hope's father says his age is at least one-half of Hope's age plus three times Hope's age. If Hope is 12, which inequality shows Hope's father's age?

F $a \geq 30$

G $a \geq 36$

H $a \geq 42$

J $a \geq 72$

Practice Test B

DIRECTIONS: Read each question and choose the best answer. Use the answer sheet provided at the end of the workbook to record your answers. If the correct answer is not available, mark the letter for "Not Here."

1. The blueprint scale shown in the table below is 3 cm:2 m.

Blueprint	3	8	b	18
Actual	2	a	10	c

Which of the following is correct for a, b, and c?

A

a	b	c
5.33	15	12

B

a	b	c
5.33	12	15

C

a	b	c
15	5.33	12

D

a	b	c
12	15	5.33

2. A coin is flipped 20 times. Which experimental probability is most consistent with the theoretical probability?

F 11 heads and 9 tails

G 13 heads and 7 tails

H 0 heads and 20 tails

J 5 heads and 15 tails

3. The table below contains a proportional relationship.

Time (d)	1	2	3	4
Distance (mi)	4	a	b	c

What are the values of a, b, and c?

A

a	b	c
8	14	16

B

a	b	c
8	12	16

C

a	b	c
10	15	20

D

a	b	c
8	14	20

4. A company has 3,000 employees. The company confirms that it will employ an additional 25% by the end of the next 5-year period. What is the average growth in number of employees per year?

F 150

G 750

H 759

J 3,750

5. The table shows a proportional relationship.

Time (min)	1	4	8	12
Distance (ft)	7	28	56	a

What is the value of a?

A 77   **B** 84   **C** 86   **D** 91

6. Look at the graph.

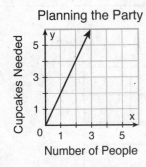

Planning the Party

Which is the correct equation for the line shown in the graph?

F $y = \frac{1}{2}x$

G $x = \frac{1}{2}y$

H $y = 2x$

J $y = x$

7. The table below shows Juanita's scores on a series of math tests.

Tests	1	2	3	4	5	6	7	8
Scores	85	92	76	100	98	50	86	80

What is her average score?

A 50

B 4.111…

C 83.375

D 95.285

8. If a plane intersects a pyramid, which of the following figures CANNOT be a cross section?

F square

G oval

H rectangle

J triangle

9. There are 5 black marbles and 3 red marbles in a bag. If marbles are drawn at random, what is the probability of NOT getting a red marble?

A $\frac{1}{5}$

B $\frac{1}{3}$

C $\frac{3}{8}$

D $\frac{5}{8}$

10. Walter's store sells outdoor grills. The end-of-season sale is advertising a 33% reduction on all grills. If the original price of grills ranges between $99.00 and $300.00 before the sale, what is the price range on sale?

F $32.67 to $99.00

G $49.50 to $150.00

H $66.33 to $201.00

J $95.73 to $290.00

11. A random sample of a shipment of nuts and bolts shows 15 out of 75 sets are missing either the bolt or the nut. What proportion could help find the number of imperfect units in a shipment of 1,000?

A $\frac{15}{75} = \frac{1,000}{x}$

B $\frac{15}{1,000} = \frac{x}{75}$

C $\frac{15}{75} = \frac{x}{1,000}$

D $\frac{1,000}{75} = \frac{15}{x}$

12. The highest point in South America is a mountain named Aconcagua in Argentina. It is 22,841 feet high. The lowest point is Laguna del Carbón, also in Argentina. It is −344 feet. How far is it from the top of Aconcagua to the bottom of Laguna del Carbón?

F −23,185 feet

G −22,497 feet

H 22,497 feet

J 23,185 feet

13. Marcie sells hats for $40.00, $60.00, and $75.00. How much does she make if she sells an equal number (n) of each hat?

A 100n

B 115n

C 135n

D 175n

14. Kermit buys and sells TVs. He charges a fee of 25% on each item he sells. If he pays $721.87 for a TV, what is his selling price?

F $240.73

G $902.34

H $1,263.27

J $1,804.67

15. Helen tossed a number cube onto a black and white chessboard. What is the probability it will land with a value equal to or less than 5 on a white square?

A $\frac{1}{3}$

B $\frac{5}{12}$

C $\frac{7}{6}$

D $\frac{5}{3}$

16. What is the probability of choosing a vowel at random from the word CONSTANTINOPLE, if each letter is written on a separate piece of paper?

F $\frac{1}{7}$ **G** $\frac{3}{14}$ **H** $\frac{5}{14}$ **J** $\frac{9}{14}$

17. Which of the following is NOT true for the expression $4\frac{7}{8} \times -15$?

A The product can be found by combining $-15(4 + \frac{7}{8})$ and will be positive.

B The product is $-73\frac{1}{8}$.

C The product will be found by combining $-15 \times \frac{39}{8}$, and the product will be negative.

D The product will be the same as $-15(4\frac{7}{8})$ and will be negative.

18. Elisa is developing a probability simulation and has created a table showing 10 trials. She determines that the 2 will measure her outcomes.

Trial	Random Numbers	Outcomes
1	2 5 9 9 1	1
2	3 2 7 0 4	1
3	8 2 1 9 5	1
4	6 6 6 7 4	0
5	4 3 4 0 3	0
6	2 6 6 7 5	1
7	0 3 1 8 5	0
8	5 9 5 6 8	0
9	0 4 7 5 2	1
10	1 1 7 3 6	0

What is the experimental probability of getting at least one 2 in a trial?

F 0.3   **H** 0.5

G 0.4   **J** 0.6

19. On a map, the distance between Los Angeles, California, and San Francisco, California, is 3 inches. The actual distance is 381 miles. What is the scale being used on the map?

A 1 in.:63.5 mi

B 1 in.:95.25 mi

C 1 in.:127 mi

D 1 in.:190 mi

20. Look at the graph below.

Which inequality is shown by the graph?

F $x > -4$

G $x < -4$

H $x \le -4$

J $x \ge -4$

21. Each box of craft paper is $10.95. The table below shows the number of boxes and the total cost of each box. Which of the following is true about the data in the table?

Boxes	1	3	5	7
Total Cost	$10.95	$32.85	$54.75	$76.65

A The total cost is always $10.95 greater than the number of the boxes.

B The ratio of the number of boxes to the total cost is 10.95.

C The ratio of the total cost to the number of boxes is 10.95.

D The number of boxes is always 10.95 times the total cost.

22. A car wash washes 20 cars in 45 minutes. What proportion would you use to find the unit rate per hour?

F $\frac{45}{20} = \frac{x}{60}$

G $\frac{20}{45} = \frac{x}{60}$

H $\frac{20}{45} = \frac{x}{1}$

J $\frac{20}{45} = \frac{1}{x}$

23. Dorothy is hanging a picture on a wall and wants to center the picture. The picture is 24 inches wide. The wall is 8 feet long. How many inches will there be between the corner of the wall and the edge of the picture?

A 24 inches

B 30 inches

C 36 inches

D 40 inches

24. George is driving from San Francisco, California, to Washington, D.C., a distance of 2,817 miles. If he drives between 300 and 400 miles per day, what is the maximum number of days the trip will take?

F a little less than 9 days

G a little more than 9 days

H a little less than 7 days

J a little more than 7 days

25. Josie's apple pie recipe calls for $3\frac{1}{2}$ cups of flour and 8 apples. How many cups of flour will she need if she uses 16 apples?

A 4.5 cups

B 7 cups

C 7.2 cups

D 11.5 cups

26. Joel buys and sells MP3 players. He purchases 75 MP3 players for $1,500.00. His markup is 33%. What is his selling price for each MP3 player?

F $2.20

G $6.60

H $20.66

J $26.60

27. Which figure will never have a rectangle as a cross section?

A cone

B cube

C prism

D cylinder

28. Hana has a basket of different-colored balls. She removes a ball at random from the basket and records the results. She puts the ball back into the basket. She repeats this experiment several times and records her results in a table like the one below.

Color	Frequency
Black	25
Red	17
Pink	21
Blue	18

What is the experimental probability of selecting a pink ball?

F $\dfrac{17}{81}$

G $\dfrac{7}{27}$

H $\dfrac{25}{81}$

J $\dfrac{20}{27}$

29. Is $\dfrac{7}{0}$ a rational number? Choose the best answer.

A No, 7 is a negative integer.

B Yes, it represents the quotient of two integers.

C No, you cannot divide by 0.

D Yes, both 7 and 0 are integers.

30. Which of the following statements is true?

F $(6 + 9.5) + -8 > 6 + (9.5 - 8)$

G $(6 + 9.5) + -8 = 6 + (9.5 - 8)$

H $(6 + 9.5) + -8 \neq 6 + (9.5 - 8)$

J $(6 + 9.5) - 8 > 6 + (9.5 - 8)$

31. Nasir is paid $1,350.00 per month, plus a commission of 2.5% of his monthly sales. His current sales are $12,360.00. How much is he paid this month?

A $275.25

B $1,041.00

C $1,316.25

D $1,659.00

32. Let p equal the price of an MP3 player. There is a sales tax of 8.75%. Which expression represents the total price paid for 3 MP3 players, including sales tax?

F $p + 1.0875p$

G $3(p + 0.0875p)$

H $3p + 0.875p$

J $3(p - 1.0875p)$

33. The width of a rectangle is 4 feet shorter than its length. Which of the following is the perimeter of the rectangle?

A $2l - 8$

B $4l - 8$

C $4l + 8$

D $2l + 8$

34. Look at the graph.

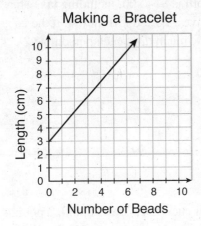

Making a Bracelet

Which of the following tells why the graph is NOT a proportional relationship?

F The value of y should decrease as the value of x increases.

G The line in the graph does not go through $(0, 0)$.

H The scale on the x-axis does not match the scale on the y-axis.

J The graph does not go through $(1, 1)$.

35. Which of the following is an example of a number and its additive inverse?

A $5 + |5| = 0$

B $5 + -5 = 0$

C $5 + |-5| = 0$

D $5 + |-5| > 0$

36. Is $7\frac{1}{3}$ a rational number? Why or why not?

F Yes, it can be expressed as 7.667.

G No, the decimal form is 7.666…, and a rational number cannot have a repeating decimal.

H No, the number is greater than 1.

J Yes, the decimal form is 7.333…, and a rational number can have a repeating decimal.

37. The diameter of a circular garden is 35 feet. A gardener is using a machine to dig a trench all around the garden. His machine moves at 16 feet per hour. About how long will it take to dig around the garden? Use $\pi = 3.14$.

A 3.43 hours

B 6.87 hours

C 19.14 hours

D Not Here

38. Sally is making $13.50 per hour. She expects a cost-of-living increase of 3%. How much will she make in a 40-hour week at the new rate?

F $523.80

G $556.20

H $588.00

J Not Here

39. The diameter of a circle is 12 cm. What will the area be if the diameter is doubled?

A 24π

B 36π

C 144π

D 576π

40. Look at the figure below.

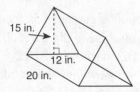

15 in.

12 in.

20 in.

What is the volume of the prism?

F 720 in.³

G 810 in.³

H 1,800 in.³

J 1,920 in.³

41. Kalia has 5 red hats and 6 blue hats. If she picks one hat at random 100 times, how many times can she expect to get a blue hat?

A 16.6

B 20

C 45.45

D 54.54

42. Five friends are having dinner at a restaurant. The total bill is $140.00, including tax. They want to leave a 20% tip. If they split the cost evenly, how much does each person pay?

F $28.50

G $32.15

H $33.60

J $42.75

43. A pound of cucumbers costs $3.50, 2 pounds cost $7.00, and 6 pounds cost $21.00. Which equation gives the total cost of x pounds of cucumbers?

A $y = 7x$

B $y = x$

C $y = \dfrac{x}{3.5}$

D $y = 3.5x$

44. The football stadium has seats in the areas listed in the table below.

Type of Seats	Number
Boxes	20
Reserved	25,000
General Admission	35,000
End Zone	8,000

Suppose all the boxes and reserved seats are sold. Which inequality will determine how many seats remain to be sold?

F $43,000 + s \leq 68,020$

G $68,020 + s \leq 43,000$

H $43,000 + s \geq 68,020$

J $25,020 + s \leq 68,020$

45. The principal wants to know if there is any interest in forming a school band. Which of the following provides the best random sample for her survey?

A asking the students in the third grade

B asking every third student in the school as they enter or leave on a particular day

C asking the students who have brothers or sisters in the school

D asking the students who take the bus to school

46. Look at the figure below.

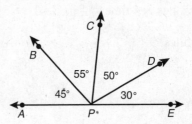

Which angles are supplementary?

F $\angle APB$ and $\angle APC$

G $\angle APD$ and $\angle DPE$

H $\angle APC$ and $\angle APD$

J $\angle BPE$ and $\angle BPD$

47. A file downloads from the Internet at a constant speed of 154 KB per second. Which of the following will NOT appear on the graph for this proportional relationship?

A (4, 631)

B (3, 462)

C (5, 770)

D (6, 924)

48. Find the sum of $16\frac{3}{8} + (-24\frac{6}{7})$.

F $-41\frac{13}{56}$

G $-8\frac{27}{56}$

H $8\frac{27}{56}$

J $41\frac{13}{56}$

49. The scale on a map is $1\frac{1}{2}$ in. equals 50 miles. How many miles is 4 times $1\frac{1}{2}$ inches?

  A 18.75 miles

  B 200 miles

  C 250 miles

  D 300 miles

50. Look at the figure below.

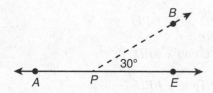

Which of the following is NOT true?

  F $\angle APB$ and $\angle BPE$ are supplementary.

  G $\angle APB$ and $\angle BPE$ are complementary.

  H $\angle APB$ equals 150°.

  J $\angle BPE$ is an acute angle.

51. Each locker in the health club has a combination lock that works with 3 digits. What is the probability that someone will choose 111 if he or she can choose from the digits 1, 2, and 3?

  A $\frac{1}{3}$

  B $\frac{3}{27}$

  C $\frac{1}{27}$

  D $\frac{2}{81}$

52. What are the mean and MAD for the following numbers: 8, 16, 46, 20, 32, 9, and 17?

  F Mean = 21.14, and MAD = 21.14.

  G Mean = 10.20, and MAD = 10.20.

  H Mean = 21.24, and MAD = 10.20.

  J Mean = 10.20, and MAD = 21.14.

53. The volume of a pyramid with a square base is 600 cubic feet. The height is 15 feet. How long is each side of the square base?

  A 10

  B $\sqrt{120}$

  C $\sqrt{3,000}$

  D 60

54. Bruce said it takes 20 minutes to complete a page of math homework. He creates the following table.

Homework (pages)	1	2	3	4
Time (min)	20	40	60	80

Which of the following is NOT true for these data?

F The table does not show a proportional relationship.

G The ratios are the same for all table entries.

H The unit rate is 20.

J The table shows a proportional relationship.

55. Given three line segments measuring 10, 5, and 20 inches, which of the following statements is true?

A The line segments form a unique triangle.

B The line segments form many similar triangles.

C The line segments form two congruent triangles.

D The line segments do not form a triangle.

56. People living in different parts of the world calculate the mean and MAD of their average temperatures. In one country, the mean is 90°F and the MAD is 2.3. In the other country, the mean is 85°F and the MAD is 10.5. What inference CANNOT be made from the data?

F The MAD of 2.3 means there is little variability in the temperatures of Country 1.

G Country 2 is always cooler than Country 1, but not by much.

H Country 2 has considerable variability in temperatures.

J There is a significant difference in temperature variability between Countries 1 and 2.

57. Emilia walks at the rate of 3 miles in $\frac{3}{5}$ hour. What is her unit rate?

A 0.2 mi/h

B 1.8 mi/h

C 3.6 mi/h

D 5 mi/h

58. A manufacturer packages items in boxes that measure 3 in. × 4 in. × 5 in. If he packages these boxes in larger shipping cartons for shipping, what is the minimum size of shipping carton he will need to hold 100 small boxes plus 5 cubic inches of packing material?

F 5,950 in.³

G 6,000 in.³

H 6,005 in.³

J 7,205 in.³

59. The scouts are helping to pack 275 boxes of canned goods for the food drive. They figure they have packed $\frac{7}{8}$ of the boxes. How many boxes are left to pack?

A 18

B 35

C 87

D 240

60. The known angles of a triangle are 42° and 48°. Which equation will give the measure of the third angle?

F $a = 90 = 48$

G $a = 180 - (42 - 48)$

H $a = 90 - 42$

J $a = 180 - (42 + 48)$

Answer Sheets

Pretest

1 Ⓐ Ⓑ Ⓒ Ⓓ	11 Ⓐ Ⓑ Ⓒ Ⓓ	21 Ⓐ Ⓑ Ⓒ Ⓓ	31 Ⓐ Ⓑ Ⓒ Ⓓ	41 Ⓐ Ⓑ Ⓒ Ⓓ	51 Ⓐ Ⓑ Ⓒ Ⓓ
2 Ⓕ Ⓖ Ⓗ Ⓙ	12 Ⓕ Ⓖ Ⓗ Ⓙ	22 Ⓕ Ⓖ Ⓗ Ⓙ	32 Ⓕ Ⓖ Ⓗ Ⓙ	42 Ⓕ Ⓖ Ⓗ Ⓙ	52 Ⓕ Ⓖ Ⓗ Ⓙ
3 Ⓐ Ⓑ Ⓒ Ⓓ	13 Ⓐ Ⓑ Ⓒ Ⓓ	23 Ⓐ Ⓑ Ⓒ Ⓓ	33 Ⓐ Ⓑ Ⓒ Ⓓ	43 Ⓐ Ⓑ Ⓒ Ⓓ	53 Ⓐ Ⓑ Ⓒ Ⓓ
4 Ⓕ Ⓖ Ⓗ Ⓙ	14 Ⓕ Ⓖ Ⓗ Ⓙ	24 Ⓕ Ⓖ Ⓗ Ⓙ	34 Ⓕ Ⓖ Ⓗ Ⓙ	44 Ⓕ Ⓖ Ⓗ Ⓙ	54 Ⓕ Ⓖ Ⓗ Ⓙ
5 Ⓐ Ⓑ Ⓒ Ⓓ	15 Ⓐ Ⓑ Ⓒ Ⓓ	25 Ⓐ Ⓑ Ⓒ Ⓓ	35 Ⓐ Ⓑ Ⓒ Ⓓ	45 Ⓐ Ⓑ Ⓒ Ⓓ	55 Ⓐ Ⓑ Ⓒ Ⓓ
6 Ⓕ Ⓖ Ⓗ Ⓙ	16 Ⓕ Ⓖ Ⓗ Ⓙ	26 Ⓕ Ⓖ Ⓗ Ⓙ	36 Ⓕ Ⓖ Ⓗ Ⓙ	46 Ⓕ Ⓖ Ⓗ Ⓙ	56 Ⓕ Ⓖ Ⓗ Ⓙ
7 Ⓐ Ⓑ Ⓒ Ⓓ	17 Ⓐ Ⓑ Ⓒ Ⓓ	27 Ⓐ Ⓑ Ⓒ Ⓓ	37 Ⓐ Ⓑ Ⓒ Ⓓ	47 Ⓐ Ⓑ Ⓒ Ⓓ	57 Ⓐ Ⓑ Ⓒ Ⓓ
8 Ⓕ Ⓖ Ⓗ Ⓙ	18 Ⓕ Ⓖ Ⓗ Ⓙ	28 Ⓕ Ⓖ Ⓗ Ⓙ	38 Ⓕ Ⓖ Ⓗ Ⓙ	48 Ⓕ Ⓖ Ⓗ Ⓙ	58 Ⓕ Ⓖ Ⓗ Ⓙ
9 Ⓐ Ⓑ Ⓒ Ⓓ	19 Ⓐ Ⓑ Ⓒ Ⓓ	29 Ⓐ Ⓑ Ⓒ Ⓓ	39 Ⓐ Ⓑ Ⓒ Ⓓ	49 Ⓐ Ⓑ Ⓒ Ⓓ	59 Ⓐ Ⓑ Ⓒ Ⓓ
10 Ⓕ Ⓖ Ⓗ Ⓙ	20 Ⓕ Ⓖ Ⓗ Ⓙ	30 Ⓕ Ⓖ Ⓗ Ⓙ	40 Ⓕ Ⓖ Ⓗ Ⓙ	50 Ⓕ Ⓖ Ⓗ Ⓙ	60 Ⓕ Ⓖ Ⓗ Ⓙ

Ratios and Proportional Relationships Modeled Instruction

1 Ⓐ Ⓑ Ⓒ Ⓓ	6 Ⓕ Ⓖ Ⓗ Ⓙ	11 Ⓐ Ⓑ Ⓒ Ⓓ	16 Ⓕ Ⓖ Ⓗ Ⓙ	21 Ⓐ Ⓑ Ⓒ Ⓓ
2 Ⓕ Ⓖ Ⓗ Ⓙ	7 Ⓐ Ⓑ Ⓒ Ⓓ	12 Ⓕ Ⓖ Ⓗ Ⓙ	17 Ⓐ Ⓑ Ⓒ Ⓓ	22 Ⓕ Ⓖ Ⓗ Ⓙ
3 Ⓐ Ⓑ Ⓒ Ⓓ	8 Ⓕ Ⓖ Ⓗ Ⓙ	13 Ⓐ Ⓑ Ⓒ Ⓓ	18 Ⓕ Ⓖ Ⓗ Ⓙ	23 Ⓐ Ⓑ Ⓒ Ⓓ
4 Ⓕ Ⓖ Ⓗ Ⓙ	9 Ⓐ Ⓑ Ⓒ Ⓓ	14 Ⓕ Ⓖ Ⓗ Ⓙ	19 Ⓐ Ⓑ Ⓒ Ⓓ	24 Ⓕ Ⓖ Ⓗ Ⓙ
5 Ⓐ Ⓑ Ⓒ Ⓓ	10 Ⓕ Ⓖ Ⓗ Ⓙ	15 Ⓐ Ⓑ Ⓒ Ⓓ	20 Ⓕ Ⓖ Ⓗ Ⓙ	25 Ⓐ Ⓑ Ⓒ Ⓓ

Ratios and Proportional Relationships Independent Practice

26 Ⓕ Ⓖ Ⓗ Ⓙ	35 Ⓐ Ⓑ Ⓒ Ⓓ	44 Ⓕ Ⓖ Ⓗ Ⓙ	53 Ⓐ Ⓑ Ⓒ Ⓓ	62 Ⓕ Ⓖ Ⓗ Ⓙ	71 Ⓐ Ⓑ Ⓒ Ⓓ
27 Ⓐ Ⓑ Ⓒ Ⓓ	36 Ⓕ Ⓖ Ⓗ Ⓙ	45 Ⓐ Ⓑ Ⓒ Ⓓ	54 Ⓕ Ⓖ Ⓗ Ⓙ	63 Ⓐ Ⓑ Ⓒ Ⓓ	72 Ⓕ Ⓖ Ⓗ Ⓙ
28 Ⓕ Ⓖ Ⓗ Ⓙ	37 Ⓐ Ⓑ Ⓒ Ⓓ	46 Ⓕ Ⓖ Ⓗ Ⓙ	55 Ⓐ Ⓑ Ⓒ Ⓓ	64 Ⓕ Ⓖ Ⓗ Ⓙ	73 Ⓐ Ⓑ Ⓒ Ⓓ
29 Ⓐ Ⓑ Ⓒ Ⓓ	38 Ⓕ Ⓖ Ⓗ Ⓙ	47 Ⓐ Ⓑ Ⓒ Ⓓ	56 Ⓕ Ⓖ Ⓗ Ⓙ	65 Ⓐ Ⓑ Ⓒ Ⓓ	74 Ⓕ Ⓖ Ⓗ Ⓙ
30 Ⓕ Ⓖ Ⓗ Ⓙ	39 Ⓐ Ⓑ Ⓒ Ⓓ	48 Ⓕ Ⓖ Ⓗ Ⓙ	57 Ⓐ Ⓑ Ⓒ Ⓓ	66 Ⓕ Ⓖ Ⓗ Ⓙ	75 Ⓐ Ⓑ Ⓒ Ⓓ
31 Ⓐ Ⓑ Ⓒ Ⓓ	40 Ⓕ Ⓖ Ⓗ Ⓙ	49 Ⓐ Ⓑ Ⓒ Ⓓ	58 Ⓕ Ⓖ Ⓗ Ⓙ	67 Ⓐ Ⓑ Ⓒ Ⓓ	
32 Ⓕ Ⓖ Ⓗ Ⓙ	41 Ⓐ Ⓑ Ⓒ Ⓓ	50 Ⓕ Ⓖ Ⓗ Ⓙ	59 Ⓐ Ⓑ Ⓒ Ⓓ	68 Ⓕ Ⓖ Ⓗ Ⓙ	
33 Ⓐ Ⓑ Ⓒ Ⓓ	42 Ⓕ Ⓖ Ⓗ Ⓙ	51 Ⓐ Ⓑ Ⓒ Ⓓ	60 Ⓕ Ⓖ Ⓗ Ⓙ	69 Ⓐ Ⓑ Ⓒ Ⓓ	
34 Ⓕ Ⓖ Ⓗ Ⓙ	43 Ⓐ Ⓑ Ⓒ Ⓓ	52 Ⓕ Ⓖ Ⓗ Ⓙ	61 Ⓐ Ⓑ Ⓒ Ⓓ	70 Ⓕ Ⓖ Ⓗ Ⓙ	

The Number System Modeled Instruction

1 Ⓐ Ⓑ Ⓒ Ⓓ	6 Ⓕ Ⓖ Ⓗ Ⓙ	11 Ⓐ Ⓑ Ⓒ Ⓓ	16 Ⓕ Ⓖ Ⓗ Ⓙ	21 Ⓐ Ⓑ Ⓒ Ⓓ
2 Ⓕ Ⓖ Ⓗ Ⓙ	7 Ⓐ Ⓑ Ⓒ Ⓓ	12 Ⓕ Ⓖ Ⓗ Ⓙ	17 Ⓐ Ⓑ Ⓒ Ⓓ	22 Ⓕ Ⓖ Ⓗ Ⓙ
3 Ⓐ Ⓑ Ⓒ Ⓓ	8 Ⓕ Ⓖ Ⓗ Ⓙ	13 Ⓐ Ⓑ Ⓒ Ⓓ	18 Ⓕ Ⓖ Ⓗ Ⓙ	23 Ⓐ Ⓑ Ⓒ Ⓓ
4 Ⓕ Ⓖ Ⓗ Ⓙ	9 Ⓐ Ⓑ Ⓒ Ⓓ	14 Ⓕ Ⓖ Ⓗ Ⓙ	19 Ⓐ Ⓑ Ⓒ Ⓓ	24 Ⓕ Ⓖ Ⓗ Ⓙ
5 Ⓐ Ⓑ Ⓒ Ⓓ	10 Ⓕ Ⓖ Ⓗ Ⓙ	15 Ⓐ Ⓑ Ⓒ Ⓓ	20 Ⓕ Ⓖ Ⓗ Ⓙ	25 Ⓐ Ⓑ Ⓒ Ⓓ

The Number System Independent Practice

26 (F) (G) (H) (J)   35 (A) (B) (C) (D)   44 (F) (G) (H) (J)   53 (A) (B) (C) (D)   62 (F) (G) (H) (J)   71 (A) (B) (C) (D)
27 (A) (B) (C) (D)   36 (F) (G) (H) (J)   45 (A) (B) (C) (D)   54 (F) (G) (H) (J)   63 (A) (B) (C) (D)   72 (F) (G) (H) (J)
28 (F) (G) (H) (J)   37 (A) (B) (C) (D)   46 (F) (G) (H) (J)   55 (A) (B) (C) (D)   64 (F) (G) (H) (J)   73 (A) (B) (C) (D)
29 (A) (B) (C) (D)   38 (F) (G) (H) (J)   47 (A) (B) (C) (D)   56 (F) (G) (H) (J)   65 (A) (B) (C) (D)   74 (F) (G) (H) (J)
30 (F) (G) (H) (J)   39 (A) (B) (C) (D)   48 (F) (G) (H) (J)   57 (A) (B) (C) (D)   66 (F) (G) (H) (J)   75 (A) (B) (C) (D)
31 (A) (B) (C) (D)   40 (F) (G) (H) (J)   49 (A) (B) (C) (D)   58 (F) (G) (H) (J)   67 (A) (B) (C) (D)
32 (F) (G) (H) (J)   41 (A) (B) (C) (D)   50 (F) (G) (H) (J)   59 (A) (B) (C) (D)   68 (F) (G) (H) (J)
33 (A) (B) (C) (D)   42 (F) (G) (H) (J)   51 (A) (B) (C) (D)   60 (F) (G) (H) (J)   69 (A) (B) (C) (D)
34 (F) (G) (H) (J)   43 (A) (B) (C) (D)   52 (F) (G) (H) (J)   61 (A) (B) (C) (D)   70 (F) (G) (H) (J)

Expressions and Equations Modeled Instruction

1 (A) (B) (C) (D)   6 (F) (G) (H) (J)   11 (A) (B) (C) (D)   16 (F) (G) (H) (J)   21 (A) (B) (C) (D)
2 (F) (G) (H) (J)   7 (A) (B) (C) (D)   12 (F) (G) (H) (J)   17 (A) (B) (C) (D)   22 (F) (G) (H) (J)
3 (A) (B) (C) (D)   8 (F) (G) (H) (J)   13 (A) (B) (C) (D)   18 (F) (G) (H) (J)   23 (A) (B) (C) (D)
4 (F) (G) (H) (J)   9 (A) (B) (C) (D)   14 (F) (G) (H) (J)   19 (A) (B) (C) (D)   24 (F) (G) (H) (J)
5 (A) (B) (C) (D)   10 (F) (G) (H) (J)   15 (A) (B) (C) (D)   20 (F) (G) (H) (J)   25 (A) (B) (C) (D)

Expressions and Equations Independent Practice

26 (F) (G) (H) (J)   35 (A) (B) (C) (D)   44 (F) (G) (H) (J)   53 (A) (B) (C) (D)   62 (F) (G) (H) (J)   71 (A) (B) (C) (D)
27 (A) (B) (C) (D)   36 (F) (G) (H) (J)   45 (A) (B) (C) (D)   54 (F) (G) (H) (J)   63 (A) (B) (C) (D)   72 (F) (G) (H) (J)
28 (F) (G) (H) (J)   37 (A) (B) (C) (D)   46 (F) (G) (H) (J)   55 (A) (B) (C) (D)   64 (F) (G) (H) (J)   73 (A) (B) (C) (D)
29 (A) (B) (C) (D)   38 (F) (G) (H) (J)   47 (A) (B) (C) (D)   56 (F) (G) (H) (J)   65 (A) (B) (C) (D)   74 (F) (G) (H) (J)
30 (F) (G) (H) (J)   39 (A) (B) (C) (D)   48 (F) (G) (H) (J)   57 (A) (B) (C) (D)   66 (F) (G) (H) (J)   75 (A) (B) (C) (D)
31 (A) (B) (C) (D)   40 (F) (G) (H) (J)   49 (A) (B) (C) (D)   58 (F) (G) (H) (J)   67 (A) (B) (C) (D)
32 (F) (G) (H) (J)   41 (A) (B) (C) (D)   50 (F) (G) (H) (J)   59 (A) (B) (C) (D)   68 (F) (G) (H) (J)
33 (A) (B) (C) (D)   42 (F) (G) (H) (J)   51 (A) (B) (C) (D)   60 (F) (G) (H) (J)   69 (A) (B) (C) (D)
34 (F) (G) (H) (J)   43 (A) (B) (C) (D)   52 (F) (G) (H) (J)   61 (A) (B) (C) (D)   70 (F) (G) (H) (J)

Geometry Modeled Instruction

1 (A) (B) (C) (D)   6 (F) (G) (H) (J)   11 (A) (B) (C) (D)   16 (F) (G) (H) (J)   21 (A) (B) (C) (D)
2 (F) (G) (H) (J)   7 (A) (B) (C) (D)   12 (F) (G) (H) (J)   17 (A) (B) (C) (D)   22 (F) (G) (H) (J)
3 (A) (B) (C) (D)   8 (F) (G) (H) (J)   13 (A) (B) (C) (D)   18 (F) (G) (H) (J)   23 (A) (B) (C) (D)
4 (F) (G) (H) (J)   9 (A) (B) (C) (D)   14 (F) (G) (H) (J)   19 (A) (B) (C) (D)   24 (F) (G) (H) (J)
5 (A) (B) (C) (D)   10 (F) (G) (H) (J)   15 (A) (B) (C) (D)   20 (F) (G) (H) (J)   25 (A) (B) (C) (D)

Geometry Independent Practice

26 (F) (G) (H) (J)   35 (A) (B) (C) (D)   44 (F) (G) (H) (J)   53 (A) (B) (C) (D)   62 (F) (G) (H) (J)   71 (A) (B) (C) (D)
27 (A) (B) (C) (D)   36 (F) (G) (H) (J)   45 (A) (B) (C) (D)   54 (F) (G) (H) (J)   63 (A) (B) (C) (D)   72 (F) (G) (H) (J)
28 (F) (G) (H) (J)   37 (A) (B) (C) (D)   46 (F) (G) (H) (J)   55 (A) (B) (C) (D)   64 (F) (G) (H) (J)   73 (A) (B) (C) (D)
29 (A) (B) (C) (D)   38 (F) (G) (H) (J)   47 (A) (B) (C) (D)   56 (F) (G) (H) (J)   65 (A) (B) (C) (D)   74 (F) (G) (H) (J)
30 (F) (G) (H) (J)   39 (A) (B) (C) (D)   48 (F) (G) (H) (J)   57 (A) (B) (C) (D)   66 (F) (G) (H) (J)   75 (A) (B) (C) (D)
31 (A) (B) (C) (D)   40 (F) (G) (H) (J)   49 (A) (B) (C) (D)   58 (F) (G) (H) (J)   67 (A) (B) (C) (D)
32 (F) (G) (H) (J)   41 (A) (B) (C) (D)   50 (F) (G) (H) (J)   59 (A) (B) (C) (D)   68 (F) (G) (H) (J)
33 (A) (B) (C) (D)   42 (F) (G) (H) (J)   51 (A) (B) (C) (D)   60 (F) (G) (H) (J)   69 (A) (B) (C) (D)
34 (F) (G) (H) (J)   43 (A) (B) (C) (D)   52 (F) (G) (H) (J)   61 (A) (B) (C) (D)   70 (F) (G) (H) (J)

Statistics and Probability Modeled Instruction

1 Ⓐ Ⓑ Ⓒ Ⓓ	6 Ⓕ Ⓖ Ⓗ Ⓙ	11 Ⓐ Ⓑ Ⓒ Ⓓ	16 Ⓕ Ⓖ Ⓗ Ⓙ	21 Ⓐ Ⓑ Ⓒ Ⓓ
2 Ⓕ Ⓖ Ⓗ Ⓙ	7 Ⓐ Ⓑ Ⓒ Ⓓ	12 Ⓕ Ⓖ Ⓗ Ⓙ	17 Ⓐ Ⓑ Ⓒ Ⓓ	22 Ⓕ Ⓖ Ⓗ Ⓙ
3 Ⓐ Ⓑ Ⓒ Ⓓ	8 Ⓕ Ⓖ Ⓗ Ⓙ	13 Ⓐ Ⓑ Ⓒ Ⓓ	18 Ⓕ Ⓖ Ⓗ Ⓙ	23 Ⓐ Ⓑ Ⓒ Ⓓ
4 Ⓕ Ⓖ Ⓗ Ⓙ	9 Ⓐ Ⓑ Ⓒ Ⓓ	14 Ⓕ Ⓖ Ⓗ Ⓙ	19 Ⓐ Ⓑ Ⓒ Ⓓ	24 Ⓕ Ⓖ Ⓗ Ⓙ
5 Ⓐ Ⓑ Ⓒ Ⓓ	10 Ⓕ Ⓖ Ⓗ Ⓙ	15 Ⓐ Ⓑ Ⓒ Ⓓ	20 Ⓕ Ⓖ Ⓗ Ⓙ	25 Ⓐ Ⓑ Ⓒ Ⓓ

Statistics and Probability Independent Practice

26 Ⓕ Ⓖ Ⓗ Ⓙ	35 Ⓐ Ⓑ Ⓒ Ⓓ	44 Ⓕ Ⓖ Ⓗ Ⓙ	53 Ⓐ Ⓑ Ⓒ Ⓓ	62 Ⓕ Ⓖ Ⓗ Ⓙ	71 Ⓐ Ⓑ Ⓒ Ⓓ
27 Ⓐ Ⓑ Ⓒ Ⓓ	36 Ⓕ Ⓖ Ⓗ Ⓙ	45 Ⓐ Ⓑ Ⓒ Ⓓ	54 Ⓕ Ⓖ Ⓗ Ⓙ	63 Ⓐ Ⓑ Ⓒ Ⓓ	72 Ⓕ Ⓖ Ⓗ Ⓙ
28 Ⓕ Ⓖ Ⓗ Ⓙ	37 Ⓐ Ⓑ Ⓒ Ⓓ	46 Ⓕ Ⓖ Ⓗ Ⓙ	55 Ⓐ Ⓑ Ⓒ Ⓓ	64 Ⓕ Ⓖ Ⓗ Ⓙ	73 Ⓐ Ⓑ Ⓒ Ⓓ
29 Ⓐ Ⓑ Ⓒ Ⓓ	38 Ⓕ Ⓖ Ⓗ Ⓙ	47 Ⓐ Ⓑ Ⓒ Ⓓ	56 Ⓕ Ⓖ Ⓗ Ⓙ	65 Ⓐ Ⓑ Ⓒ Ⓓ	74 Ⓕ Ⓖ Ⓗ Ⓙ
30 Ⓕ Ⓖ Ⓗ Ⓙ	39 Ⓐ Ⓑ Ⓒ Ⓓ	48 Ⓕ Ⓖ Ⓗ Ⓙ	57 Ⓐ Ⓑ Ⓒ Ⓓ	66 Ⓕ Ⓖ Ⓗ Ⓙ	75 Ⓐ Ⓑ Ⓒ Ⓓ
31 Ⓐ Ⓑ Ⓒ Ⓓ	40 Ⓕ Ⓖ Ⓗ Ⓙ	49 Ⓐ Ⓑ Ⓒ Ⓓ	58 Ⓕ Ⓖ Ⓗ Ⓙ	67 Ⓐ Ⓑ Ⓒ Ⓓ	
32 Ⓕ Ⓖ Ⓗ Ⓙ	41 Ⓐ Ⓑ Ⓒ Ⓓ	50 Ⓕ Ⓖ Ⓗ Ⓙ	59 Ⓐ Ⓑ Ⓒ Ⓓ	68 Ⓕ Ⓖ Ⓗ Ⓙ	
33 Ⓐ Ⓑ Ⓒ Ⓓ	42 Ⓕ Ⓖ Ⓗ Ⓙ	51 Ⓐ Ⓑ Ⓒ Ⓓ	60 Ⓕ Ⓖ Ⓗ Ⓙ	69 Ⓐ Ⓑ Ⓒ Ⓓ	
34 Ⓕ Ⓖ Ⓗ Ⓙ	43 Ⓐ Ⓑ Ⓒ Ⓓ	52 Ⓕ Ⓖ Ⓗ Ⓙ	61 Ⓐ Ⓑ Ⓒ Ⓓ	70 Ⓕ Ⓖ Ⓗ Ⓙ	

Practice Test A

1 Ⓐ Ⓑ Ⓒ Ⓓ	11 Ⓐ Ⓑ Ⓒ Ⓓ	21 Ⓐ Ⓑ Ⓒ Ⓓ	31 Ⓐ Ⓑ Ⓒ Ⓓ	41 Ⓐ Ⓑ Ⓒ Ⓓ	51 Ⓐ Ⓑ Ⓒ Ⓓ
2 Ⓕ Ⓖ Ⓗ Ⓙ	12 Ⓕ Ⓖ Ⓗ Ⓙ	22 Ⓕ Ⓖ Ⓗ Ⓙ	32 Ⓕ Ⓖ Ⓗ Ⓙ	42 Ⓕ Ⓖ Ⓗ Ⓙ	52 Ⓕ Ⓖ Ⓗ Ⓙ
3 Ⓐ Ⓑ Ⓒ Ⓓ	13 Ⓐ Ⓑ Ⓒ Ⓓ	23 Ⓐ Ⓑ Ⓒ Ⓓ	33 Ⓐ Ⓑ Ⓒ Ⓓ	43 Ⓐ Ⓑ Ⓒ Ⓓ	53 Ⓐ Ⓑ Ⓒ Ⓓ
4 Ⓕ Ⓖ Ⓗ Ⓙ	14 Ⓕ Ⓖ Ⓗ Ⓙ	24 Ⓕ Ⓖ Ⓗ Ⓙ	34 Ⓕ Ⓖ Ⓗ Ⓙ	44 Ⓕ Ⓖ Ⓗ Ⓙ	54 Ⓕ Ⓖ Ⓗ Ⓙ
5 Ⓐ Ⓑ Ⓒ Ⓓ	15 Ⓐ Ⓑ Ⓒ Ⓓ	25 Ⓐ Ⓑ Ⓒ Ⓓ	35 Ⓐ Ⓑ Ⓒ Ⓓ	45 Ⓐ Ⓑ Ⓒ Ⓓ	55 Ⓐ Ⓑ Ⓒ Ⓓ
6 Ⓕ Ⓖ Ⓗ Ⓙ	16 Ⓕ Ⓖ Ⓗ Ⓙ	26 Ⓕ Ⓖ Ⓗ Ⓙ	36 Ⓕ Ⓖ Ⓗ Ⓙ	46 Ⓕ Ⓖ Ⓗ Ⓙ	56 Ⓕ Ⓖ Ⓗ Ⓙ
7 Ⓐ Ⓑ Ⓒ Ⓓ	17 Ⓐ Ⓑ Ⓒ Ⓓ	27 Ⓐ Ⓑ Ⓒ Ⓓ	37 Ⓐ Ⓑ Ⓒ Ⓓ	47 Ⓐ Ⓑ Ⓒ Ⓓ	57 Ⓐ Ⓑ Ⓒ Ⓓ
8 Ⓕ Ⓖ Ⓗ Ⓙ	18 Ⓕ Ⓖ Ⓗ Ⓙ	28 Ⓕ Ⓖ Ⓗ Ⓙ	38 Ⓕ Ⓖ Ⓗ Ⓙ	48 Ⓕ Ⓖ Ⓗ Ⓙ	58 Ⓕ Ⓖ Ⓗ Ⓙ
9 Ⓐ Ⓑ Ⓒ Ⓓ	19 Ⓐ Ⓑ Ⓒ Ⓓ	29 Ⓐ Ⓑ Ⓒ Ⓓ	39 Ⓐ Ⓑ Ⓒ Ⓓ	49 Ⓐ Ⓑ Ⓒ Ⓓ	59 Ⓐ Ⓑ Ⓒ Ⓓ
10 Ⓕ Ⓖ Ⓗ Ⓙ	20 Ⓕ Ⓖ Ⓗ Ⓙ	30 Ⓕ Ⓖ Ⓗ Ⓙ	40 Ⓕ Ⓖ Ⓗ Ⓙ	50 Ⓕ Ⓖ Ⓗ Ⓙ	60 Ⓕ Ⓖ Ⓗ Ⓙ

Practice Test B

1 Ⓐ Ⓑ Ⓒ Ⓓ	11 Ⓐ Ⓑ Ⓒ Ⓓ	21 Ⓐ Ⓑ Ⓒ Ⓓ	31 Ⓐ Ⓑ Ⓒ Ⓓ	41 Ⓐ Ⓑ Ⓒ Ⓓ	51 Ⓐ Ⓑ Ⓒ Ⓓ
2 Ⓕ Ⓖ Ⓗ Ⓙ	12 Ⓕ Ⓖ Ⓗ Ⓙ	22 Ⓕ Ⓖ Ⓗ Ⓙ	32 Ⓕ Ⓖ Ⓗ Ⓙ	42 Ⓕ Ⓖ Ⓗ Ⓙ	52 Ⓕ Ⓖ Ⓗ Ⓙ
3 Ⓐ Ⓑ Ⓒ Ⓓ	13 Ⓐ Ⓑ Ⓒ Ⓓ	23 Ⓐ Ⓑ Ⓒ Ⓓ	33 Ⓐ Ⓑ Ⓒ Ⓓ	43 Ⓐ Ⓑ Ⓒ Ⓓ	53 Ⓐ Ⓑ Ⓒ Ⓓ
4 Ⓕ Ⓖ Ⓗ Ⓙ	14 Ⓕ Ⓖ Ⓗ Ⓙ	24 Ⓕ Ⓖ Ⓗ Ⓙ	34 Ⓕ Ⓖ Ⓗ Ⓙ	44 Ⓕ Ⓖ Ⓗ Ⓙ	54 Ⓕ Ⓖ Ⓗ Ⓙ
5 Ⓐ Ⓑ Ⓒ Ⓓ	15 Ⓐ Ⓑ Ⓒ Ⓓ	25 Ⓐ Ⓑ Ⓒ Ⓓ	35 Ⓐ Ⓑ Ⓒ Ⓓ	45 Ⓐ Ⓑ Ⓒ Ⓓ	55 Ⓐ Ⓑ Ⓒ Ⓓ
6 Ⓕ Ⓖ Ⓗ Ⓙ	16 Ⓕ Ⓖ Ⓗ Ⓙ	26 Ⓕ Ⓖ Ⓗ Ⓙ	36 Ⓕ Ⓖ Ⓗ Ⓙ	46 Ⓕ Ⓖ Ⓗ Ⓙ	56 Ⓕ Ⓖ Ⓗ Ⓙ
7 Ⓐ Ⓑ Ⓒ Ⓓ	17 Ⓐ Ⓑ Ⓒ Ⓓ	27 Ⓐ Ⓑ Ⓒ Ⓓ	37 Ⓐ Ⓑ Ⓒ Ⓓ	47 Ⓐ Ⓑ Ⓒ Ⓓ	57 Ⓐ Ⓑ Ⓒ Ⓓ
8 Ⓕ Ⓖ Ⓗ Ⓙ	18 Ⓕ Ⓖ Ⓗ Ⓙ	28 Ⓕ Ⓖ Ⓗ Ⓙ	38 Ⓕ Ⓖ Ⓗ Ⓙ	48 Ⓕ Ⓖ Ⓗ Ⓙ	58 Ⓕ Ⓖ Ⓗ Ⓙ
9 Ⓐ Ⓑ Ⓒ Ⓓ	19 Ⓐ Ⓑ Ⓒ Ⓓ	29 Ⓐ Ⓑ Ⓒ Ⓓ	39 Ⓐ Ⓑ Ⓒ Ⓓ	49 Ⓐ Ⓑ Ⓒ Ⓓ	59 Ⓐ Ⓑ Ⓒ Ⓓ
10 Ⓕ Ⓖ Ⓗ Ⓙ	20 Ⓕ Ⓖ Ⓗ Ⓙ	30 Ⓕ Ⓖ Ⓗ Ⓙ	40 Ⓕ Ⓖ Ⓗ Ⓙ	50 Ⓕ Ⓖ Ⓗ Ⓙ	60 Ⓕ Ⓖ Ⓗ Ⓙ

Answer Key

Pretest

1. A [7.RP.2.c]

2. G [7.RP.3]

3. C [7.RP.2.b]

4. H [7.RP.1]

5. A [7.RP.3]

6. H [7.RP.2.a]

7. C [7.RP.2.a]

8. F [7.RP.2.c]

9. D [7.RP.2.d]

10. G [7.RP.2.d]

11. D [7.RP.1]

12. G [7.RP.3]

13. A [7.NS.1.a]

14. G [7.NS.1.b]

15. A [7.NS.2.c]

16. J [7.NS.2.a]

17. D [7.NS.2.d]

18. H [7.NS.1.c]

19. A [7.NS.1.d]

20. H [7.NS.2.d]

21. D [7.NS.2.b]

22. F [7.NS.2.c]

23. C [7.NS.3]

24. G [7.NS.3]

25. A [7.EE.1]

26. H [7.EE.2]

27. C [7.EE.3]

28. H [7.EE.4.a]

29. D [7.EE.4.b]

30. F [7.EE.1]

31. D [7.EE.2]

32. G [7.EE.3]

33. B [7.EE.4.a]

34. J [7.EE.4.b]

35. B [7.EE.4.a]

36. F [7.EE.1]

37. A [7.G.1]

38. H [7.G.2]

39. D [7.G.3]

40. G [7.G.4]

41. A [7.G.5]

42. G [7.G.6]

43. C [7.G.1]

44. J [7.G.2]

45. C [7.G.3]

46. G [7.G.4]

47. B [7.G.5]

48. G [7.G.6]

49. C [7.SP.1]

50. G [7.SP.2]

51. D [7.SP.3]

52. F [7.SP.4]

53. D [7.SP.5]

54. G [7.SP.6]

55. D [7.SP.7.a]

56. F [7.SP.7.b]

57. D [7.SP.8.a]

58. G [7.SP.8.b]

59. D [7.SP.8.a]

60. F [7.SP.8.c]

Ratios and Proportional Relationships

Modeled Instruction

1. C [7.RP.2.d]

2. G [7.RP.1]

3. D [7.RP.2.b]

4. H [7.RP.2.d]

5. D [7.RP.2.c]

6. J [7.RP.1]

7. B [7.RP.2.c]

8. G [7.RP.2.a]

9. B [7.RP.2.d]

10. F [7.RP.2.b]

11. D [7.RP.2.d]

12. F [7.RP.3]

13. B [7.RP.1]

14. H [7.RP.1]

15. D [7.RP.1]

16. G [7.RP.3]

17. D [7.RP.2.b]

18. G [7.RP.2.c]

19. D [7.RP.3]

20. H [7.RP.2.c]

21. A [7.RP.2.a]

22. G [7.RP.2.a]

23. D [7.RP.2.a]

24. H [7.RP.2.b]

25. C [7.RP.3]

Ratios and Proportional Relationships

Independent Practice

26. J [7.RP.2.d]

27. B [7.RP.1]

28. J [7.RP.2.d]

29. A [7.RP.2.a]

30. H [7.RP.2.a]

31. D [7.RP.1]

32. H [7.RP.3]

33. B [7.RP.3]

34. G [7.RP.1]

35. B [7.RP.2.d]

36. H [7.RP.2.c]

37. A [7.RP.2.b]

38. H [7.RP.3]

39. D [7.RP.2.b]

40. J [7.RP.1]

41. B [7.RP.3]

42. H [7.RP.2.d]

43. C [7.RP.2.a]

44. G [7.RP.2.c]

45. B [7.RP.1]

46. J [7.RP.1]

47. A [7.RP.2.b]

48. H [7.RP.2.a]

49. B [7.RP.2.c]

50. J [7.RP.1]

51. A [7.RP.2.b]

52. J [7.RP.2.a]

53. B [7.RP.1]

54. G [7.RP.2.c]

55. D [7.RP.2.c]

56. G [7.RP.3]

57. D [7.RP.2.d]

58. G [7.RP.2.b]

59. D [7.RP.2.d]

60. F [7.RP.2.c]

61. B [7.RP.2.d]

62. G [7.RP.1]

63. B [7.RP.2.a]

64. H [7.RP.2.a]

65. C [7.RP.2.b]

66. G [7.RP.3]

67. C [7.RP.2.a]

68. J [7.RP.2.b]

69. A [7.RP.3]

70. G [7.RP.2.c]

71. B [7.RP.3]

72. H [7.RP.2.d]

73. C [7.RP.3]

74. G [7.RP.2.c]

75. C [7.RP.2.b]

The Number System
Modeled Instruction

1. A [7.NS.2.b]

2. G [7.NS.2.d]

3. B [7.NS.1.d]

4. G [7.NS.1.b]

5. C [7.NS.1.a]

6. J [7.NS.2.a]

7. A [7.NS.2.c]

8. F [7.NS.2.b]

9. D [7.NS.2.a]

10. G [7.NS.1.a]

11. A [7.NS.1.d]

12. G [7.NS.1.b]

13. B [7.NS.1.d]

14. F [7.NS.2.b]

15. C [7.NS.3]

16. F [7.NS.1.c]

17. B [7.NS.1.b]

18. J [7.NS.2.a]

19. D [7.NS.2.c]

20. H [7.NS.1.c]

21. C [7.NS.2.d]

22. F [7.NS.1.c]

23. C [7.NS.3]

24. H [7.NS.2.d]

25. A [7.NS.3]

The Number System
Independent Practice

26. H [7.NS.1.b]

27. A [7.NS.2.a]

28. J [7.NS.2.d]

29. A [7.NS.2.b]

30. F [7.NS.2.c]

31. B [7.NS.3]

32. H [7.NS.1.a]

33. B [7.NS.2.b]

34. G [7.NS.1.d]

35. B [7.NS.2.d]

36. F [7.NS.1.b]

37. D [7.NS.1.b]

38. G [7.NS.1.c]

39. B [7.NS.3]

40. J [7.NS.1.a]

41. C [7.NS.2.d]

42. J [7.NS.2.a]

43. B [7.NS.2.a]

44. J [7.NS.1.d]

45. C [7.NS.3]

46. J [7.NS.2.c]

47. B [7.NS.2.a]

48. J [7.NS.2.d]

49. D [7.NS.1.c]

50. H [7.NS.2.c]

51. A [7.NS.2.b]

52. G [7.NS.3]

53. D [7.NS.1.d]

54. G [7.NS.2.b]

55. D [7.NS.1.a]

56. F [7.NS.1.d]

57. B [7.NS.2.c]

58. F [7.NS.1.c]

59. C [7.NS.2.b]

60. F [7.NS.1.d]

61. A [7.NS.2.c]

62. G [7.NS.1.a]

63. A [7.NS.2.d]

64. F [7.NS.2.a]

65. A [7.NS.1.d]

66. J [7.NS.1.b]

67. C [7.NS.1.b]

68. J [7.NS.1.c]

69. A [7.NS.1.c]

70. G [7.NS.2.c]

71. A [7.NS.3]

72. F [7.NS.1.b]

73. B [7.NS.1.b]

74. G [7.NS.3]

75. B [7.NS.2.d]

**Expressions and Equations
Modeled Instruction**

1. B [7.EE.3]

2. H [7.EE.4.b]

3. D [7.EE.2]

4. H [7.EE.4.a]

5. B [7.EE.4.a]

6. F [7.EE.2]

7. D [7.EE.1]

8. G [7.EE.3]

9. C [7.EE.4.b]

10. F [7.EE.1]

11. D [7.EE.2]

12. F [7.EE.4.a]

13. A [7.EE.3]

14. G [7.EE.4.a]

15. D [7.EE.4.b]

16. H [7.EE.1]

17. D [7.EE.2]

18. F [7.EE.3]

19. B [7.EE.1]

20. J [7.EE.2]

21. C [7.EE.3]

22. G [7.EE.4.a]

23. A [7.EE.1]

24. G [7.EE.4.b]

25. B [7.EE.4.b]

**Expressions and Equations
Independent Practice**

26. G [7.EE.2]

27. C [7.EE.4.a]

28. H [7.EE.3]

29. B [7.EE.1]

30. J [7.EE.1]

31. C [7.EE.2]

32. F [7.EE.4.a]

33. B [7.EE.4.b]

34. G [7.EE.4.a]

35. C [7.EE.2]

36. G [7.EE.3]

37. D [7.EE.1]

38. G [7.EE.3]

39. A [7.EE.4.b]

40. F [7.EE.4.a]

41. B [7.EE.3]

42. J [7.EE.1]

43. D [7.EE.4.a]

44. H [7.EE.1]

45. B [7.EE.4.b]

46. H [7.EE.1]

47. C [7.EE.3]

48. H [7.EE.4.b]

49. C [7.EE.1]

50. J [7.EE.4.b]

51. D [7.EE.4.b]

52. G [7.EE.3]

53. A [7.EE.2]

54. G [7.EE.3]

55. C [7.EE.1]

56. G [7.EE.4.a]

57. B [7.EE.1]

58. G [7.EE.2]

59. C [7.EE.3]

60. H [7.EE.2]

61. B [7.EE.2]

62. J [7.EE.2]

63. B [7.EE.4.a]

64. J [7.EE.4.b]

65. D [7.EE.2]

66. H [7.EE.4.a]

67. A [7.EE.4.a]

68. H [7.EE.4.a]

69. A [7.EE.4.b]

70. G [7.EE.3]

71. B [7.EE.2]

72. G [7.EE.2]

73. C [7.EE.1]

74. J [7.EE.3]

75. D [7.EE.2]

**Geometry
Modeled Instruction**

1. B [7.G.6]

2. H [7.G.4]

3. C [7.G.5]

4. G [7.G.6]

5. C [7.G.3]

6. G [7.G.1]

7. C [7.G.6]

8. J [7.G.5]

9. B [7.G.6]

10. H [7.G.4]

11. B [7.G.1]

12. F [7.G.3]

13. D [7.G.1]

14. H [7.G.2]

15. B [7.G.6]

16. G [7.G.3]

17. B [7.G.4]

18. G [7.G.4]

19. A [7.G.5]

20. G [7.G.1]

21. D [7.G.3]

22. G [7.G.2]

23. A [7.G.5]

24. J [7.G.5]

25. C [7.G.2]

**Geometry
Independent Practice**

26. F [7.G.2]

27. B [7.G.6]

28. J [7.G.2]

29. D [7.G.3]

30. G [7.G.1]

31. B [7.G.4]

32. H [7.G.2]

33. A [7.G.6]

34. G [7.G.5]

35. A [7.G.6]

36. J [7.G.4]

37. A [7.G.5]

38. G [7.G.3]

39. A [7.G.3]

40. H [7.G.3]

41. D [7.G.1]

42. G [7.G.4]

43. B [7.G.3]

44. G [7.G.5]

45. B [7.G.1]

46. F [7.G.6]

47. B [7.G.2]

48. J [7.G.4]

49. B [7.G.4]

50. G [7.G.6]

51. C [7.G.1]

52. H [7.G.4]

53. B [7.G.2]

54. G [7.G.1]

55. A [7.G.5]

56. G [7.G.3]

57. A [7.G.4]

58. H [7.G.1]

59. C [7.G.6]

60. F [7.G.5]

61. C [7.G.6]

62. H [7.G.2]

63. D [7.G.1]

64. H [7.G.5]

65. D [7.G.1]

66. J [7.G.5]

67. C [7.G.6]

68. G [7.G.6]

69. B [7.G.5]

70. J [7.G.5]

71. A [7.G.4]

72. G [7.G.6]

73. A [7.G.4]

74. J [7.G.6]

75. C [7.G.2]

Statistics and Probability Modeled Instruction

1. C [7.SP.1]

2. F [7.SP.3]

3. B [7.SP.5]

4. J [7.SP.8.b]

5. C [7.SP.4]

6. G [7.SP.8.b]

7. D [7.SP.5]

8. F [7.SP.2]

9. A [7.SP.7.b]

10. J [7.SP.2]

11. C [7.SP.7.a]

12. J [7.SP.6]

13. A [7.SP.4]

14. G [7.SP.1]

15. B [7.SP.8.a]

16. G [7.SP.3]

17. B [7.SP.3]

18. H [7.SP.8.c]

19. A [7.SP.8.a]

20. G [7.SP.7.a]

21. B [7.SP.6]

22. H [7.SP.1]

23. D [7.SP.7.b]

24. J [7.SP.2]

25. A [7.SP.4]

Statistics and Probability Independent Practice

26. F [7.SP.7.a]

27. D [7.SP.3]

28. F [7.SP.1]

29. C [7.SP.6]

30. G [7.SP.5]

31. B [7.SP.6]

32. F [7.SP.5]

33. B [7.SP.7.a]

34. J [7.SP.8.b]

35. C [7.SP.4]

36. G [7.SP.3]

37. C [7.SP.3]

38. J [7.SP.5]

39. A [7.SP.7.a]

40. H [7.SP.4]

41. C [7.SP.8.b]

42. J [7.SP.2]

43. C [7.SP.8.b]

44. J [7.SP.2]

45. A [7.SP.7.b]

46. H [7.SP.6]

47. D [7.SP.3]

48. H [7.SP.1]

49. C [7.SP.8.a]

50. G [7.SP.1]

51. B [7.SP.6]

52. F [7.SP.8.a]

53. B [7.SP.7.b]

54. G [7.SP.5]

55. B [7.SP.4]

56. H [7.SP.7.a]

57. B [7.SP.2]

58. G [7.SP.7.b]

59. C [7.SP.1]

60. G [7.SP.8.a]

61. D [7.SP.8.a]

62. F [7.SP.3]

63. B [7.SP.1]

64. G [7.SP.7.a]

65. D [7.SP.8.b]

66. H [7.SP.5]

67. A [7.SP.4]

68. H [7.SP.2]

69. A [7.SP.4]

70. H [7.SP.8.c]

71. C [7.SP.7.b]

72. H [7.SP.7.b]

73. D [7.SP.8.a]

74. H [7.SP.6]

75. A [7.SP.2]

Practice Test A

1. B [7.NS.1.b]
2. F [7.RP.1]
3. D [7.EE.2]
4. H [7.EE.1]
5. A [7.G.2]
6. J [7.SP.8.b]
7. B [7.NS.1.d]
8. H [7.RP.2.c]
9. B [7.EE.4.a]
10. G [7.NS.2.d]
11. C [7.G.6]
12. F [7.NS.2.d]
13. B [7.EE.4.a]
14. J [7.SP.1]
15. B [7.RP.3]
16. G [7.RP.2.b]
17. B [7.EE.3]
18. F [7.EE.4.a]
19. C [7.G.6]
20. G [7.RP.2.d]
21. A [7.G.5]
22. G [7.NS.2.b]
23. C [7.SP.8.a]
24. G [7.SP.5]
25. B [7.NS.3]
26. G [7.RP.1]
27. D [7.NS.2.c]
28. G [7.SP.4]
29. B [7.NS.2.a]
30. H [7.SP.3]
31. A [7.RP.2.b]
32. F [7.EE.4.b]
33. C [7.G.5]
34. H [7.G.1]
35. C [7.RP.2.c]
36. F [7.G.3]
37. C [7.G.1]
38. H [7.EE.4.b]
39. A [7.SP.6]
40. H [7.EE.2]
41. C [7.RP.2.d]
42. G [7.SP.8.c]
43. B [7.G.2]
44. G [7.G.4]
45. C [7.RP.3]
46. H [7.NS.3]
47. C [7.G.3]
48. J [7.RP.2.a]
49. D [7.G.4]
50. F [7.EE.3]
51. C [7.NS.1.d]
52. J [7.SP.8.b]
53. A [7.SP.2]
54. F [7.EE.1]
55. C [7.SP.7.b]
56. G [7.SP.7.a]
57. B [7.NS.1.a]
58. F [7.RP.2.a]
59. B [7.NS.1.c]
60. H [7.EE.4.b]

Practice Test B

1. A [7.G.1]
2. F [7.SP.7.a]
3. B [7.RP.2.a]
4. F [7.EE.3]
5. B [7.RP.2.b]
6. H [7.RP.2.c]
7. C [7.NS.3]
8. G [7.G.3]
9. D [7.SP.5]
10. H [7.EE.2]
11. C [7.SP.2]
12. J [7.NS.1.c]
13. D [7.EE.2]
14. G [7.EE.2]
15. B [7.SP.8.a]
16. H [7.SP.8.a]
17. A [7.NS.2.a]
18. H [7.SP.8.c]
19. C [7.G.1]
20. J [7.EE.4.b]
21. C [7.RP.2.b]
22. G [7.RP.1]
23. C [7.EE.3]
24. G [7.NS.2.c]
25. B [7.NS.2.b]
26. J [7.EE.4.a]
27. A [7.G.3]
28. G [7.SP.7.b]
29. C [7.NS.2.b]
30. G [7.NS.1.d]
31. D [7.RP.3]
32. G [7.EE.1]
33. B [7.EE.1]
34. G [7.RP.2.d]
35. B [7.NS.1.a]
36. J [7.NS.2.d]
37. B [7.G.4]
38. G [7.EE.3]
39. C [7.G.4]
40. H [7.G.6]
41. D [7.SP.6]
42. H [7.RP.3]
43. D [7.RP.2.c]
44. J [7.EE.4.b]
45. B [7.SP.1]
46. G [7.G.5]
47. A [7.RP.2.d]
48. G [7.NS.1.b]
49. B [7.NS.2.c]
50. G [7.G.2]
51. C [7.SP.8.b]
52. H [7.SP.3]
53. B [7.EE.4.a]
54. F [7.RP.2.a]
55. D [7.G.2]
56. G [7.SP.4]
57. D [7.RP.1]
58. H [7.G.6]
59. B [7.NS.2.a]
60. J [7.G.5]

Reference Sheet

Length

Customary

1 mile (mi) = 5,280 feet (ft)

1 mile (mi) = 1,760 yards (yd)

1 yard (yd) = 3 feet (ft)

1 foot (ft) = 12 inches (in.)

Metric

1 kilometer (km) = 1,000 meters (m)

1 meter (m) = 100 centimeters (cm)

1 centimeter (cm) = 10 millimeters (mm)

Volume and Capacity

Customary

1 gallon (gal) = 128 fluid ounces (fl oz)

1 gallon (gal) = 4 quarts (qt)

1 quart (qt) = 2 pints (pt)

1 pint (pt) = 2 cups (c)

1 cup (c) = 8 fluid ounces (fl oz)

Metric

1 liter (L) = 1,000 milliliters (mL)

Weight and Mass

Customary

1 ton (T) = 2,000 pounds (lb)

1 pound (lb) = 16 ounces (oz)

Metric

1 kilogram (kg) = 1,000 grams (g)

1 gram (g) = 1,000 milligrams (mg)

Perimeter of a Rectangle	$P = 2l + 2w$

Circumference	$C = 2\pi r$ or $C = \pi d$

Area

Triangle	$A = \frac{1}{2} bh$
Rectangle	$A = bh$
Parallelogram	$A = bh$
Trapezoid	$A = \frac{1}{2}(b_1 + b_2)h$
Circle	$A = \pi r^2$

Volume

Prism	$V = Bh$
Pyramid	$V = \frac{1}{3} Bh$
Cylinder	$V = \pi r^2 h$ or $V = Bh$
Sphere	$V = \frac{4}{3}\pi r^3$

Pi

π	$\pi \approx 3.14$ or $\pi \approx \frac{22}{7}$